Thomas Jefferson Murray

Valuable Cooking Receipts

Thomas Jefferson Murray

Valuable Cooking Receipts

ISBN/EAN: 9783744788823

Printed in Europe, USA, Canada, Australia, Japan

Cover: Foto ©Lupo / pixelio.de

More available books at **www.hansebooks.com**

COOKING RECEIPTS

NEW YORK,
GEORGE W. HARLAN
19 PARK PLACE.

VALUABLE

COOKING RECEIPTS.

BY

THOMAS J. MURREY,

Late Caterer of Astor House and Rossmore Hotel of New York, and
Continental Hotel of Philadelphia.

NEW YORK:
GEORGE W. HARLAN,
19 PARK PLACE.
1880.

Copyright, 1880, by
GEORGE W. HARLAN.

PREFACE.

IN issuing this little volume the publisher is aware that the market is already deluged with "cook-books," both good and bad; but the aim in this instance is to utilize the experience of a caterer, who has spent twenty-five years of his life in the service of leading hotels and restaurants all over the country, besides catering to the appetites of thousands of private families. The well-known and unsurpassed *cuisine* of the hotels where he has been employed would of itself form testimony conclusive of his culinary ability, but he possesses besides numerous flattering letters from private parties, many of high standing in the community. As a salad-maker his reputation is wide-spread, and his receipts under this head are numbered among the hundreds, any one of which is a masterpiece of epicurean art and taste. It is my intention shortly to issue a book containing these receipts.

In writing receipts for this volume Mr. Murrey has kept economy constantly in mind, and has endeavored to present some of the most appetizing formulas in such a shape as to be within the reach of all families of moderate means. Each and every receipt has been personally tested and can be implicitly relied upon. The arrangement is that of a regular bill of fare or *ménu*. It will be understood, of course, that the contents of this book do not pretend to cover the field of cookery. Some idea of the magnitude of such a task can be had when you are informed that Mr. Murrey possesses probably the largest library on gastronomic art in this country, numbering many thousand volumes. Like all men who have made this art a study, he has aimed to so construct his formulas as to ward off indigestion and dyspepsia. Apropos at this point is a story illustrating the philanthropy of that prince of French *chefs*, Carême. Meeting one day a woman bitterly weeping at the door of a wine-shop, his commiserating question was answered by saying her husband was within; all his earnings were spent there and his family left to starve. Close questioning revealed the fact that the culprit liked good living, and that the wife condemned him to boiled beef every day. "No man cares to go abroad," said Carême reproachfully, "for a bad meal, if his wife can cook him a good one, particularly if a silversmith and earning money." Carême visited the house the next morning, and ordered a silver cup to be repaired, and, while waiting for its completion, offered to cook his own breakfast, which the man and wife shared. It was woodcock cooked in a way to electrify an Apicius. Carême called again for his cup with some wild duck. Meantime, the wife made rapid progress in the *chef's* art. The husband ceased wasting his money. The delicate fare improved his intellect; he became an artist in his trade, and finally one day Carême received a box containing a silver woodcock exquisitely carved, carrying in its beak a tiny silver cup, with the inscription, "To Carême, from a friend who was saved by good cooking."

THE PUBLISHER.

VALUABLE COOKING RECEIPTS.

OYSTERS.

Raw Oysters.—Eat raw oysters as plain and as free from condiments as possible, and always on the deep shell in their own liquor. The average American orders a dozen on the half-shell and then drowns his pets in vinegar, pepper, salt, horse-radish, etc., washing them down with some malt beverage, pays his check, and disappears. The next day he goes through the same performance, and the not over-conscientious oyster-man, knowing his weakness for condiments, can easily palm off on him a "Rockaway Cull" for a Blue Point or a Green Point, or he may give him a "deep-water native" for almost any particular kind or brand he may want, and he cannot detect the difference in their flavor, owing to his excessive use of condiments. A little lemon-juice is all that is necessary, if you will not eat your saline dainties natural.

The heartless oyster-fiend who opens your oysters by *smashing* the shell should be avoided, for it is cruelty, to say the least. We can forgive him for spattering our clothing with shells, mud, and dirty water, but filling our mouths with these things is pure ugliness. Order a quart of the bivalves to be sent home, and this oyster-butcher endangers the health of your family should any of them swallow a particle of the shell. The true lover of an oyster should have some feeling for his little favorite, and patronize establishments only where they contrive to open them (Boston fashion) so dexterously that the mollusk is hardly conscious he has been removed from his lodging "till he feels the teeth of the piscivorous gourmet tickling him to death."

Roast Oysters on half-shell.—Open a dozen large oysters on deep shell; add a walnut of butter, with a little salt and mixed pepper (red and black) and a pinch of cracker-dust to each. Place them on a broiler over a sharp, clear fire until done, and serve.

Families not having all the conveniences for roasting oysters "restaurant fashion" will find the above receip acceptable; though I must confess it is quite a treat to our Western cousins to ask them down into the kitchen of an evening, and serve up a peck of oysters roasted in the shell direct from the fire, with no other tool to pick them out of the coals than the old tongs the moment they pop open. You may possibly burn a finger or two, but what of that so long as the young folks have had a good time?

Oysters escalloped.—In a deep yellow dish place a layer of oysters and cover them with cracker-dust (add an ounce of butter to each layer of cracker-dust); pepper and salt to taste; another layer of oysters, another of cracker-dust, and so on until the dish is full. Moisten the dish with the juice of the oysters or hot water to prevent its burning, and bake a nice brown.

Oyster Patties.—Roll out some very light puff paste half an inch thick; stamp it in rounds with a cutter three inches in diameter; press a small cutter two inches in diameter on the middle of each to the depth of a quarter of an inch. Place the rounds on a buttered tin, baste them lightly with egg, and bake in a quick oven. When done take them out, remove the centre-piece, scoop out a little of the inside, and fill the shells with the prepared oysters.

Parboil twenty-five oysters in their own liquor; remove the oysters and season the liquid with lemon-peel, nutmeg, and pepper; strain, and thicken with a heaping tablespoonful of flour, one and a half ounces of butter, a wineglassful of rich cream; mix, and then add the oysters. Simmer all together a few minutes, fill the shells, and serve.

Scallops and clams cut up fine, with a sauce made on the same principle, make a very nice patty.

Valuable Cooking Receipts.

Oyster toast.—Select fifteen plump oysters; mince them, and season with mixed pepper and a pinch of nutmeg; beat the yolks of four eggs and mix them with half a pint of cream. Put the whole into a saucepan and set it over the fire to simmer till thick; stir it well, and do not let it boil lest it should curdle. Toast five pieces of bread and butter them; when your dish is near boiling-point remove it from the fire and pour it over the toast.

Fried oysters.—Beat up the yolks of four eggs with three tablespoonfuls of sweet oil, and season them with a teaspoonful of salt and a salt-spoonful of cayenne pepper; beat up thoroughly. Dry twelve fat oysters on a napkin; dip them in the egg-batter, then in cracker-dust; shake off the loose cracker-dust, dip them again in the egg-batter, and lastly roll them in fine *bread-crumbs.* Fry in very hot fat, using fat enough to cover them. The oil gives them a nice flavor. (Private receipt of a prominent Philadelphia caterer.)

Broiled oysters.—Rub the bars of a wire broiler with a little sweet butter. Dry twelve large, fat oysters and place them upon the broiler *plain.* Broil them over a clear fire, and when done on both sides send to table on a piece of buttered toast, with a little melted butter in a separate dish. Should you *hanker* after a delightful case of dyspepsia cover them with egg-batter and roll them in crumbs before broiling.

Oysters a la Poulette.—Blanch a dozen oysters in their own liquor; salt and remove the oysters; add a tablespoonful of butter, the juice of half a lemon, a gill of cream, and a teaspoonful of flour. Beat up the yolk of one egg while the sauce is simmering; add the egg, and simmer the whole until it thickens. Place the oysters on a hot dish, pour the sauce over them, sprinkle a little chopped parsley on top, and send to table. (This is a favorite dish of Hotel Brunswick *habitués* in New York.)

SOUPS.

Sir Henry Thompson says "that soups, whether clear or thick, are far too lightly esteemed by most classes. They are too often regarded as the mere prelude to a meal, to be swallowed hastily or disregarded altogether." And the *Almanach des Gourmands* tells us that ten folio volumes would not contain the receipts of all the soups that have been invented in the Parisian kitchen alone.

Soup Stock.—In making soups from raw meats break the bones apart, place them in a pot, cover them with *cold water*, and boil slowly for five or six hours; add salt to quicken the rising of the scum, which should be thoroughly removed. Cut up three carrots, three turnips, two heads of celery, and two onions; add to the stock, together with six or eight cloves, a bouquet of herbs, and a teaspoonful of whole peppers; strain into a deep saucepan, and clarify with the white of egg. It will then be ready for an indefinite variety of soups.

Veal Stock.—Chop up three slices of bacon and two pounds of the neck of veal; place in a stew-pan with a pint of water or beef stock, and simmer half an hour; then add two quarts of stock, one onion, a carrot, a bouquet of herbs, four stalks of celery, half a teaspoonful of bruised whole peppers, and a pinch of nutmeg with a teaspoonful of salt; boil gently for two hours, removing the scum in the meantime. Strain into an earthern crock, and when cold remove the fat. A few bones of poultry added, with an additional quantity of water or stock, will improve it.

Veal Broth.—Stew a knuckle of veal in about three quarts of water; add two ounces of rice, a little salt, and a blade of mace; boil until the liquor is reduced one-half.

Gumbo Soup.—Cut up two chickens, two slices of ham, and two onions into dice; flour them, and fry the whole to a light brown; then fill the frying-pan with boiling water, stir it a few minutes, and turn the whole into a saucepan containing three quarts of boiling water; let it boil forty minutes, removing the scum. In the meantime soak three pints of ochra in cold water twenty minutes; cut them into thin slices, and add to the other ingredients; let it boil one hour and a half. Add a quart of canned tomatoes and a cupful of boiled rice half an hour before serving.

Southern housekeepers use the leaves of the sassafras-tree as a substitute for ochra when the latter is scarce and dear. They gather the young leaves and spread them in the shade for a few days; then they dry them in the sun. When they are thoroughly dried they put them in a bag and hang them up for two or three months; they are then pulverized and bottled.

Mock Turtle Soup.—Take half a calf's head with the skin on; remove the brains. Wash the head in several waters, and let it soak in cold water for an hour. Put it in a saucepan with five quarts of beef stock; let it simmer gently for an hour; remove the scum carefully, take up the head, let it get cold, and cut the meat from the bones into pieces an inch square and set them in the ice-box. Dissolve two ounces of butter in a frying-pan; mince a large onion and fry it in the butter until nicely browned, and add to the stock in which the head was cooked. Return the bones to the stock; simmer the soup, removing the scum until no more rises. Put in a carrot, a turnip, a bunch of parsley, a bouquet of herbs, a dozen outer stalks of celery, two blades of mace, and the rind of one lemon, grated; salt and pepper to taste. Boil gently for two hours, and strain the soup through a flannel cloth. Mix three ounces of Barlow's prepared browned flour with a pint of the soup, and simmer until it thickens; then add it to the soup. Take the pieces of head out of the ice-box and add to the soup; let them simmer until quite tender. "Before serving add a little Worcestershire sauce, a tablespoonful of anchovy paste, a gobletful of port or sherry, and two lemons sliced, each slice cut into quarters with the rind trimmed off." Warm the wine a very little before adding it to the soup. Keep in ice-box three or four days before using. Serve the brains as a side-dish.

Pea Soup.—Cut two large slices of ham into dice with a sliced onion, and fry them in a little bacon fat until they are lightly browned. Cut up one turnip, one large carrot, four outer stalks of celery, and one leek into small pieces; add these last ingredients to the ham and onion, and let them simmer for fifteen minutes; then pour over them three quarts of corned-beef water or hot water, and add a pint of split peas which have been soaked in cold water all night; boil gently until the peas are quite tender, stirring constantly to prevent burning; then add salt and pepper to taste, with a teaspoonful of brown sugar. Remove the soup from the fire and rub through a sieve; if it is not thick enough to suit your taste or fancy add a few ounces of flour mixed smoothly in a little cold milk; return the soup to the fire, and simmer for half an hour. Cut up four slices of American bread into small dice, and fry the pieces in very hot fat until nicely browned; place them on a napkin or towel, and add a few of them to each plate or tureen of soup just before it goes to table.

Economical Pea Soup.—Boil two quarts of green-pea hulls in four quarts of water, in which beef, mutton, or fowl has been boiled, four hours; then add a bunch or bouquet of herbs, salt and pepper, a tablespoonful of butter, and a quart of milk. Rub through a hair-sieve, thicken with a little flour, and serve with croutons, as in the foregoing receipt.

Tomato Soup.—Cut four ounces of ham into dice; slice two onions and fry with ham in two ounces of butter; when browned turn them into a saucepan containing three quarts of stock or corned-beef water, and add three carrots, two turnips, one red pepper (lady-finger), and a dozen outer stalks of celery; simmer gently for one hour, then add a quart of canned tomatoes; boil gently for another hour, rub the whole through a sieve, and simmer again with the liquor a few minutes; add salt and serve with croutons.

Oxtail Soup.—Take two oxtails; cut them into joints, and cut up each joint into four pieces; put them into a pan with two ounces of butter, and fry them ten minutes. Slice two onions, one turnip, two carrots, a dozen outer stalks of celery, and fry in the same butter, with three slices of bacon cut up fine; fry to a light brown. Turn the ingredients into a saucepan with a quart of stock or ham-water, and boil quickly for half an hour; then add two more quarts of stock, a bouquet of herbs, two bay-leaves, a dozen whole peppers crushed, a few cloves, and salt to taste.

Simmer until the meat is quite tender; then take it out, strain the soup, skim off the fat, and thicken with two ounces of Barlow's prepared flour; return the meat to the soup, add a tablespoonful of Worcestershire, a cupful of sherry, and serve with grated rusks.

Chicken Soup.—Take three young male chickens; cut them up, put them in a saucepan with three quarts of veal stock; a sliced carrot, one turnip, and one head of celery may be put with them and removed before the soup is thickened. Let them simmer for an hour. Remove all the white flesh; return the rest of the birds to the soup, and boil gently for two hours. Pour a little of the liquid over a quarter of a pound of the crumbs of bread, and when they are well soaked put it in a mortar with the white flesh of the birds, and pound the whole to a smooth paste; add a pinch of ground mace, salt, and a little cayenne pepper, press the mixture through a sieve, and boil once more, adding a pint of boiling cream; thicken with a very little flour mixed in cold milk, remove the bones, and serve.

Chicken Soup, No. 2.—Cut up one chicken; put into a stew-pan two quarts of cold water, a teaspoonful of salt, and one pod of red pepper (lady-finger); when half done add two dessert-spoonfuls of well-washed rice. When thoroughly cooked remove the bird from the soup, tear a part of the breast into shreds (saving the balance of the fowl for a salad), and add it to the soup with a wineglassful of cream.

Beef Tea.—Take half a pound of lean beef; cut it up into small bits; let it soak in a pint of water three-quarters of an hour, then put both into a quart champagne bottle with just a suspicion of salt; cork tightly, and wire the cork, so as to prevent its popping out. Set the bottle into a saucepanful of warm water, boil gently an hour and a half, and strain through a napkin.

Beef tea administered often to a patient without the fibrine of the meat will tend to weaken instead of strengthening the invalid. I always add about a teaspoonful of finely-chopped raw meat to a goblet of the tea, and let it stand in the tea about five minutes before serving.

FISH.

Codfish is about the best fish that comes to our market, but it is so cheap and plentiful that we do not appreciate it quite as much as we would if the price was twenty-five cents a pound and its *season* to last not over two months. Trout and all delicate fish lose their flavor long before they reach New York, and they should be eaten within half an hour after they are caught; while the cod improves in flavor if kept for a day or two with the addition of a little salt to give it firmness.

The "shoulder part" pleases *my* palate the most. Have you ever tried a codfish steak for breakfast, dredged in cornmeal and fried in salt pork-fat? It is splendid. A rasher of bacon served with it does no harm.

In broiling cod, haddock, bass, etc., always tie them up in a bag or towel, and lay the fish in the fish-pan, adding a little salt, a pint of Rhine wine, or cupful of vinegar, and cover the fish with *cold water*, allowing it to boil gently till done. Drawn-butter sauce with boiled fish is easy to make and pleases almost everybody.

Baked Cod.—When purchasing a four-pound cod ask your fish-dealer to send you three or four "codfish-heads," and as soon as the basket comes into the house rub a little salt on the fish, chop the heads into six pieces each, and sprinkle a little salt over them. Place them in the centre of the baking-pan (to be used as supports for the fish), with two ounces of butter, one carrot, a turnip, a potato, and one onion cut into slices, two blades of mace, a teaspoonful white pepper, one tablespoonful celery-seed, six cloves, and a cupful of red wine. Set the pan in the oven while you prepare the cod.

Soak in cold water until soft a sufficiency of bread to fill the fish; drain off the water and pound the bread to a paste; mix with it two tablespoonfuls of melted butter, two raw eggs, a tablespoonful Worcestershire sauce, with salt and pepper to taste. Put this stuffing inside the fish and sew it up; place the cod in the pan with two or three pieces of butter on the upper side of the fish, and baste it frequently; when it is cooked lay the fish on a hot platter, and garnish with fried oysters, if convenient. Add two tablespoonfuls of Barlow's prepared flour to the pan, a wineglass of sherry; mix, and strain the gravy into a sauce-boat.

Salt Codfish with Cream.—Soak one pound and a half of salt codfish over-night. Next morning set the fish to simmer for about two hours; drain off the water and strip the fish into shreds; place it in a saucepan with a quart of milk and two ounces of butter; mix a tablespoonful of flour with two tablespoonfuls of cold milk, and add to the fish. Let the whole come to a boil, remove the dish from the fire, beat up one egg to a froth, add it to the fish, stir, and serve immediately.

Salt Mackerel Broiled.—Soak a No. 2 chicken mackerel in cold water over-night; pour off the water and let the fish stand in milk enough to cover it for one hour before broiling; baste the fish with butter, and broil. When done plunge the fish into hot water for one minute, and send to table with a dish of melted butter, the juice of one lemon, and a teaspoonful of chopped parsley mixed together.

Broiled Lobster (for breakfast).—Cut the tail part of a lobster in two, rub a little sweet-oil over the meat, and broil.

When done brush a little butter over it, with the juice of half a lemon and just the suspicion of cayenne. Place the meat back into the shell, and send to table with a dish of broiled tomatoes and a fresh-baked potato.

Lobster en Brochette.—Cut up the tail of a lobster into square pieces; take a few thin slices of bacon and cut into lengths to match the pieces of lobster; place them on a skewer alternately, and broil; baste as in "broiled lobster," and send to table on a bed of water-cress.

Baked Shad.—Make a dressing of bread-crumbs, butter, pepper, and salt worked to a paste; fill the shad with the mixture, sew it up, and place it lengthwise in a baking-pan with a little water and an ounce of butter. Fill the space between the fish and the sides of the pan with slices of raw potatoes one-fourth of an inch thick, and serve fish and potatoes together. Add a spoonful of Barlow's prepared flour to the gravy, and serve.

"Tenderloin" Trout.—Take a large catfish and cut it up into pieces two inches in length and one inch in thickness. Beat up three eggs with a little salt and pepper and a teaspoonful of Worcestershire; dip the fish in the egg-batter, and roll in corn-meal or bread-crumbs. Fry a deep brown, garnish with lemon, parsley, or celery-tops, and send to table with a cucumber salad.

Fricasseed Eels.—Cut up three pounds of eels into pieces of three inches in length; put them into a stew-pan, and cover them with Rhine wine (or two-thirds water and one-third vinegar); add fifteen oysters, two pieces of lemon, a bouquet of herbs, one onion quartered, six cloves, three stalks celery, a pinch of cayenne, pepper and salt to taste. Stew the eels one hour; remove them from the dish; strain the liquor. Put it back into the stew-pan with a gill of cream and an ounce of butter rolled in flour; simmer gently a few minutes, pour over the fish, and serve with a toasted milk cracker.

Soyer's Boiled Salmon.—I always prefer dressing this fish in slices from an inch to two inches in thickness, boiling it in plenty of salt and water twenty minutes. The whole fish may be boiled, but it requires longer boiling. Salmon eats firmer by not putting it into water until it is boiling. Dress the fish upon a napkin and serve with lobster-sauce, or plain melted butter with a few sprigs of parsley boiled a few minutes in it.

I generally boil a salmon whole, or head and shoulders in one piece, with salt, and cover the fish with equal parts of warm water and Rhine wine, two or three bay-leaves, a few cloves, etc. When done I use the water in making sauce by reducing one-half, adding butter rolled in flour to thicken, pinch of cayenne, and the juice of one lemon.

Eel Patties.—Take three medium-sized eels and cut them up into inch pieces. Put them in a stew-pan, add salt, and cover them with cold water. When the water comes to a boil take them off the fire, wash them in cold water, scrape off any fat that may adhere, return them to the stew-pan with just enough hot water to cover them, and add a blade of mace, a bay-leaf, a few whole peppers, a few sprigs of parsley, and one lemon cut into slices. Stew gently until the fish will separate from the bone; remove the fish from the broth, pick it into small pieces, and set them aside; reduce the broth a little, strain, and thicken with flour and butter. Return the fish to the broth, simmer a moment, fill your patties and serve; make patty-shells as directed for oyster patties.

Drawn-Butter Sauce.—Season a cupful of flour with salt, pepper, and a pinch of nutmeg, mix it with some water into a paste, and work in a piece of butter about the size of an egg; put the pan over the fire and boil for twenty minutes; then take it off, add some fresh butter in small portions at a time, stirring continually to prevent the butter from rising to the top. Add the juice of half a lemon before serving.

Maitre d'Hotel Butter.—Mix four ounces of butter with a heaping tablespoonful of chopped parsley, salt and pepper, and the juice of three lemons; serve with boiled fish, etc.

Anchovy Sauce.—An easy way of making anchovy sauce is to stir two or three teaspoonfuls of prepared essence or paste of anchovy (which may be bought at your grocer's) into a pint of melted butter; let the sauce boil a few minutes, and flavor with lemon-juice.

Lobster Sauce.—Break the shell of the lobster into small pieces. Pour over them one pint of water or veal-stock and a pinch of salt; simmer gently until the liquid is reduced one-half. Mix two ounces of butter with an ounce of flour, strain the liquid upon it, and stir all over the fire until the mixture thickens; do not let it boil. Add two tablespoonfuls of the lobster-meat, the juice of half a lemon, and serve.

The spawn and coral mixed with double the quantity of butter, a little cayenne, and pounded in a mortar to a paste, then pressed through a hair-sieve, is called lobster-butter; a spoonful of it added to the sauce will improve it; the rest of the butter may be used in garnishing and decorating cold salmon, etc.

Caper Sauce.—Chop up two tablespoonfuls of capers and add them to half a pint of melted butter, with the piece of one lemon, a teaspoonful Worcestershire sauce, and a pinch of cayenne; put on the fire and simmer a few minutes; mix a teaspoonful of flour with a very little cold water, and add to the sauce.

Celery Sauce.—Put two ounces of butter into a saucepan, melt it, and add two heads of celery cut up into inch pieces; stir the celery in the pan until it is quite tender; add salt and pepper, with a little mace. Mix a tablespoonful of flour in a cupful of stock and simmer half an hour. A cupful of cream may be used instead of the stock.

Oyster Sauce.—Blanch one dozen oysters in their own liquor; then take the oysters out and add two blades of mace, an ounce of melted butter, and a cupful of thickened cream; return the oysters to the sauce, let them come to a boil, and serve; salt to taste.

Oyster Sauce, No. 2.—Take a dozen large oysters and boil them in their own liquor two minutes; remove them from the liquid, and quarter them. Mix an ounce of butter and an ounce of flour in a stew-pan, add the oyster liquor, a pinch of cayenne or two drops tobasco pepper-sauce, with a little nutmeg and half a pint of cream. Stir the whole gently over the fire until the sauce is smooth and thick. Add the pieces of oysters, simmer a moment longer, and serve.

Egg Sauce.—Put two ounces of butter into a saucepan with a dessert-spoonful of flour and a very little water; simmer gently. When ready to boil take the saucepan from the fire and stir in two ounces more of butter and three cold hard-boiled eggs cut up small; sprinkle a little salt on the egg.

Dutch Sauce.—Blend together two ounces of butter and a teaspoonful of flour; put it into a stew-pan with equal quantities of stock and vinegar (from the bottle containing imported mixed pickles), say a wineglassful of each; stir for two minutes, and add the beaten yolks of two eggs, keeping up the stirring till the mixture thickens; if you let it boil it will curdle. Add the juice of half a lemon before serving.

Gravy for Baked Fish.—Brown a sliced onion in a little butter and add gradually a pint of stock; thicken with a tablespoonful of Barlow's prepared flour, and let the mixture simmer with a bunch of parsley nearly half an hour; strain the gravy and add salt and a teaspoonful walnut-catsup.

BOILING.

Before boiling joints of meat the cook should think for a moment whether she desires the juices to go into the water, as in soup, gravies, etc., or to be retained in the meat itself. If they are to be retained put the meat into fast-boiling water, and let it boil for ten minutes to make the outside hard and thus prevent the juice escaping; then add cold water equal in quantity to about one-half of the boiling water; this will reduce the temperature to about 160° (Liebig), at which point the meat (raw) should be kept until thoroughly done, which, however, takes a much longer time than the ordinary mode. Care must be taken to remove the scum when the water is on the point of boiling, or it will quickly sink and spoil the appearance of the meat.

If it is desired to extract the juice from raw meat, cover it with cold water and simmer slowly as before.

Salted meat requires longer boiling than fresh meat.

Dried and smoked meat should be soaked for some hours before it is put into the water. Place your meat in a saucepan sufficiently large to contain the joint easily and cover with water, and no more.

Boiled Leg of Mutton.—Cut off the shank-bone, trim the knuckle, and wash the mutton; put it into a pot with salt and cover with boiling water. Allow it to boil a few minutes; skim the surface clean, draw your pot to the side of the fire, and simmer until done. Time, from two to two hours and a half.

Do not *try* the leg with a fork to determine whether it is done or not. You will lose all the juices of the meat by so doing.

Serve with caper sauce, or melted butter with a few small capers added.

The liquor from the boiling may be converted into soup with the addition of a ham-bone and a few vegetables boiled together.

English housekeepers hang up a leg of mutton from two days to at least a week before using, weather allowing.

Corned Beef.—Put your corned beef in a saucepan or pot and cover with cold water; boil gently until done. Allow half an hour to the pound after it has come to a boil.

The ingredients used in making a pickle for corned beef harden the fibres of the meat, so that to plunge it into hot water would not only make it tough and hard but indigestible.

Boiled Tongue.—Soak a smoked or dry tongue over-night. Next morning set it in a pot of water and simmer slowly for five or six hours. Remove the pot from the fire, and when the water has cooled take out the tongue, tear off the skin, and trim off the ragged end.

Boiled Ham.—Soak the ham over-night; scrape off the rusty spots, put into a pot, and cover with plenty of cold water; add a bouquet of herbs and a few cloves to the water, and boil very slowly until done; remove the pot from the fire, and when cold take out the ham, take off the skin, trim the fat off around the edge. Take half a cupful of brown sugar, a teaspoonful of prepared browned flour, and moisten with port wine; cover this paste over the fat of the ham, and set it in a very hot oven until the mixture froths.

Boiled Chicken.—Wash a chicken in lukewarm water; truss it, put it into hot water, let it come to a boil, then draw it to one side of the fire and let it simmer gently until ready; remove the scum as it rises. The more slowly it boils the whiter and tenderer it will be. Add a very little salt, and half a lemon cut into small pieces, to the water before boiling. Serve with any white or cream sauce.

Boiled Turkey.—Cassell's work on cookery tells us that "there is an old proverb which says that a turkey boiled is a turkey spoiled, but in this couplet there is more rhyme than reason, as a boiled turkey forms a dainty dish, most acceptable to persons with delicate stomachs, who fear the richness of the roasted bird." Take a plump hen-turkey, singe, draw it, and truss as you would to roast; make a stuffing of herbs, salt, pepper, bread-crumbs, a little mace and grated lemon-peel, with a few oysters chopped up, a spoonful of butter, and a raw egg; mix your dressing well together, fill the bird, and sew it up; tie up the turkey in a flowered cloth to make it white, and simmer until tender. Time, about two hours and a half.

Serve with oyster sauce.

Boiled Capon.—Boil a capon as you would a large chicken, add a bouquet of herbs to the water, and serve with egg sauce.

When a boiled fowl has been so far used that meat slices cannot be carved from it, the remains may be cut up for hash, seasoned with salt and pepper, moistened with hot water (or the water in which the fowl has been boiled); stir the dish while it is simmering to prevent burning; serve on a piece of buttered toast, and place two poached eggs on top of the hash for each person. Or mince the remains of fowl very fine with an equal quantity of calf's brains or sweetbreads; season with salt, pepper, and a little nutmeg; add a little cracker-dust, two raw eggs; moisten with Rhine wine or cream, mix well together, roll into balls the size of an egg, dip into egg batter, then into crumbs, and fry in very hot fat.

ENTREES.

Fillet of Beef.—Cut the fillet (tenderloin) out of a sirloin of beef; trim off the fat and the suck or skin, and lard it with fat pork cut into narrow strips two inches long. Put each strip of pork (or bacon) into a larding-needle, and with the point of your needle take up as much flesh as will hold the strip of pork, allowing about half an inch of each end exposed after removing the needle; repeat this process as neatly and as evenly as possible and at equal distances until finished. Rub a little sweet oil and salt over the fillet; set it one side a few minutes while you prepare the roasting (baking) pan for it.

Chop up into small pieces a few beef or veal bones, and cover the bottom of your pan with them. Add three slices of bacon, two carrots, two onions, and one turnip sliced, with a pint of stock. Season with salt, bruised whole peppers, a bay-leaf, a few cloves, and a blade of mace. Place the fillet in the pan with the larded side up. Moisten it with a wineglassful of vinegar, and bake. When done remove the fillet, add a tablespoonful of Barlow's prepared flour and a glass of sherry or port to the pan, mix, and strain the sauce on to the fillet. Chop up half a dozen button-mushrooms, sprinkle over the meat, and serve.

Beef a la Mode.—Take three pounds of fresh rump of beef; remove the fat and sinews. Cut fat bacon into long strips and lard the meat with it through and through. Mix together a few cloves, mace, allspice, whole peppers, salt-spoonful of cayenne, a tablespoonful of powdered herbs, and a clove of garlic, with half a pint of vinegar. Put the meat into an earthen crock or deep stew-pan, with a thin piece of bacon under it; add the vinegar and seasoning and a pint of stock, with a walnut of butter rolled in flour. Cover the crock and simmer gently until done. When preferred vegetables may be added and served with the beef, allowing plenty of stock or water for them to boil nicely.

Beef Stew.—Take a three pound piece of rump of beef; remove the bone, bind it up tight, and put it in a pot or stew-pan that will just hold it. Season with ground spices. Fry two large onions sliced, and add them to it, with two carrots, two turnips, a few cloves, a blade of mace, a head of celery, and a potato quartered; add stock enough to cover the meat. Simmer as gently as possible until quite tender. Remove the fat, take out the meat, and add half a pint of port, a wineglassful of vinegar, a tablespoonful Worcestershire sauce to the gravy; strain over the meat, and serve with a garnish of assorted vegetables arranged neatly around the dish.

Beefsteak Pie.—Cover the sides of a raised pie-mould with butter, and put a lining of paste made in the following manner neatly into it: Chop a quarter of a pound of suet; put it into a stew-pan with the same quantity of butter and a pint of water. When boiling pass them through a sieve into two pounds of flour, and stir it with a spoon until cold. When the paste is quite smooth roll it out and it is ready for the lining. Cut up two pounds of round or rump steak into pieces about two inches square; dust them with flour; season with parsley, salt, and pepper; lay them round the mould; fill it with alternate layers of potatoes cut into quarters, and meat. Make a lid for the mould with some of the paste, brush it over with beaten egg, and bake three hours. Put an ornamental centre to the cover, that it may be more easily raised to throw in some gravy as soon as it is baked.

Calf's Head.—The first thing to do on receiving a calf's head is to remove the brains, throw them into cold water for an hour, drain, then boil them in salt and water for twenty minutes, and set them aside.

Put the head into cold water and wash it well, and leave it there to draw out the blood for an hour; then take it out and dry it well with a towel.

Bone a calf's head in the following manner: Place the calf's head on the table with the front part of the head facing you; draw the sharp point of a knife from the back part of the head right down to the nose, making an incision down to the bone of the skull; then with the knife clear the scalp and cheeks from the bones right and left, always keeping the point of the knife close to the bone. If you have not previously removed the brains, chop the head in two and remove them as carefully as possible.

When the head has been boned wash it well, wipe it with a clean cloth, season the inside with salt and pepper, roll it up with the tongue, tie it up, and blanch it in hot water for ten minutes; then put it into cold water a few minutes, wipe it dry, and set it aside until wanted.

Fried Calf's Head.—Cut the prepared calf's head into pieces two inches wide; lay them for three hours in a pickle made of two tablespoonfuls of lemon-juice, a wineglassful of Rhine wine, salt and pepper, and a pinch of mace. Take them out, drain them, and dip each piece in egg-batter; roll in cracker-dust, fry in hot fat, and send to table with sauce tartare.

Sauce Tartare.—Mince two small English pickles, one-fourth of an onion, and a few sprigs of parsley together. Add them to three tablespoonfuls of mayonnaise sauce, and the juice of half a lemon. Mix and serve (see mayonnaise sauce). A few tarragon-leaves will improve the sauce.

Calf's Head, Maitre d'Hotel.—Cut up your prepared calf's head into neat slices, and simmer gently for two hours; take out the pieces of meat, place on a hot dish, and cover them with Maitre d'Hôtel sauce; garnish with parsley.

Calf's Head Broiled.—Cut up a prepared calf's head into pieces quite three inches wide; place them in a saucepan, cover with water. Add a wineglassful of vinegar, and simmer half an hour; then place them in cold water a few minutes, dry them on a towel, rub a little sweet-oil over each piece, and broil. When done brush melted butter over them with the juice of half a lemon.

Calf's Head Collared.—Bone a calf's head carefully, wash it well, and wipe it dry; lay the head on the table, and spread on it a force-meat made of the brain and tongue, and a very little ham mixed with a tablespoonful of chopped parsley, a teaspoonful of thyme, a teaspoonful of marjoram, the minced yolks of three hard-boiled eggs, a wineglassful brandy, and a little salt, pepper, and nutmeg. Roll the head as tightly as possible, and tie it in a cloth, binding it with tape. Put it into a saucepan with stock enough to cover it, and add a carrot, a parsnip, one onion, a sliced lemon, a few bay-leaves, salt, and a dozen bruised peppers.

Let it boil gently three hours; then take it out of the cloth and pour round it a sauce made of a pint of the liquid in which it was boiled, with a little lemon-juice, two small pickles, and four button-mushrooms chopped fine.

Calf's Brains en Matelotte.—Wash the brains in several waters, remove the skin, and boil them in salt and water with a little vinegar in it for ten minutes. Take them out and lay them in cold water until wanted. Melt a tablespoonful of butter in a saucepan, and mix with it a teaspoonful of flour. Add three button-onions sliced, a teaspoonful Worcestershire, a clove, a bay-leaf, half a pint of stock, and a wineglassful of Rhine wine. When these are mixed thoroughly together put the brains with them and let them stew twenty minutes.

Calf's Brains Fried.—Prepare the brains as in the foregoing receipt. Cut them into slices, dip them in egg-batter, roll in crumbs, and fry in hot fat or butter; garnish with fried parsley.

Calf's Brains and Tongue.—Prepare the brains as heretofore recommended, and chop them. Put them in a saucepan with two tablespoonfuls of butter, a little chopped parsley, the juice of half a lemon, salt, and cayenne pepper. Skin and trim the boiled tongue, place it in the middle of the dish and pour the sauce and brains round it, and send to table.

Stewed Sweet-Breads.—Soak two sweet-breads in cold water for one hour; change the water twice; put them in boiling water ten minutes till they are firm, then take them out and place them in cold water until wanted.

Place them in a stew-pan, cover them with stock, and simmer nearly an hour; take them out, place them on a hot dish, remove the gravy from the fire a minute, and add to it gradually the yolk of an egg and four tablespoonfuls of cream; put this over a fire till the sauce thickens, but do not let it boil. Before serving add the juice of a lemon, pour the sauce around the sweet-breads, and send to table with a dish of green peas.

They may be cut up and fried after dipping in egg and rolled in crumbs.

Sweet-breads are very nice broiled and served with Maître d'Hôtel butter; garnish with parsley.

Pork Chops, Tomato Sauce.—Broil three nice pork chops, and when well done sprinkle them with pepper and salt, place on a hot dish, and serve with tomato sauce poured around them.

Tomato Sauce.—Stew half a dozen tomatoes in a pint of stock, with a slice of ham cut into dice, a bay-leaf, a blade of mace, three drops of tabasco pepper-sauce, and three small pickled onions; stir the whole over a gentle fire until done, then press them through a sieve, add salt, and put the sauce again upon the fire till it is very hot.

Pork tenderloin baked or broiled is acceptable with sauce Robert.

Sauce Robert.—Slice two onions, and fry them in butter until they begin to turn yellow; pour over them as much brown gravy as will cover them; add a tablespoonful of French or German mustard (do not use English mustard), a teaspoonful of salt, a salt-spoonful of pepper. Simmer very gently, adding more gravy, if necessary, till the onions are tender. Rub them through a fine sieve. Mix with the pulp a very little more stock or gravy, and boil once. This is a simple recipe, and one that any housekeeper can easily make.

Pork Sausages.—The most wholesome way to cook sausages is to bake them. Place them in a baking-pan in a single layer, and bake in a moderate oven; turn them over when they are half done, that they may be equally browned all over. Send to table with pieces of toast between each sausage. Cut the toast about the same size as the sausage, and moisten it with a very little of the sausage-fat.

They make a nice entrée by placing them on a mound of mashed potatoes and served with apple-sauce, or small apple-fritters neatly arranged round them.

About the best sausages that come to the New York market are the Deerfoot Farm sausages; fancy grocers retail them for about twenty cents a pound. Split them in two and broil them, and send to table with Boston brown-bread toast, buttered. Use your sausage-fat for frying hash, etc.

Breast of Mutton with Peas.—Cut up two pounds of the breast of mutton into square pieces; put them into a stew-pan with an ounce of butter, and brown them nicely; then cover with hot water and stew for an hour. Take the meat from the pan and skim all the fat from the gravy; place the meat in a clean saucepan with one onion sliced, a bouquet of herbs, pepper and salt; pour in the gravy, and stew for one hour; add a quart of young peas, remove the herbs, simmer fifteen minutes, and serve.

String beans cut into dice, or boiled macaroni, may be substituted for the peas.

Curry of Mutton.—Put six button-onions, cut fine, and an ounce of butter into a saucepan with an ounce of curry-powder, a teaspoonful of salt, a tablespoonful of flour, and half a pint of cream; stir until smooth. Remove the bones from two pounds of mutton, cut it into neat pieces, and fry a light brown; put the meat into a saucepan, pour the sauce over it, and boil gently one hour and a half. Place the meat on a hot dish and arrange a border of broiled rice neatly round it.

Cold boiled mutton cut into slices may be used instead of the raw meat.

Veal may be used instead of mutton.

Mutton Hash with Poached Eggs.—Take a pound and a half of the remains of roast mutton, chop it up fine, and put it in a stew-pan with a cupful of mutton gravy or stock; season with salt, pepper, and a little grated nutmeg; add a tablespoonful of Barlow's prepared flour, and let the meat heat gradually until hot. Do not let it boil. Simmer twenty minutes, and serve with poached eggs placed neatly round the dish.

A spoonful of Worcestershire sauce may be added to the dish, if desired.

Ragout of Mutton.—Slice two turnips, two carrots, and two onions; put them in a saucepan with two ounces of butter, and brown them. Dust in a little flour and stir the whole to prevent browning too quickly, and turn them out upon a hot dish until wanted.

Cut up cold roast mutton into square pieces, and brown them on each side in the same pan in which you browned your vegetables; then add half a pint of hot water, salt and pepper, a few sprigs of parsley, and the sliced vegetables. Stew gently until the vegetables are tender; arrange the vegetables in the centre of the dish, with the meat as a border; pour the sauce over all, and serve.

Mutton Pie.—Cut into square pieces about two pounds of cold roast or boiled mutton; trim off a portion of the fat; quarter three kidneys; put the meat into a pie dish, season with two tablespoonfuls of chopped parsley, a tablespoonful of powdered herbs, salt and pepper, and half an onion minced; add half a pint of light stock or water, a wineglassful of port wine; cover the dish with puff paste, brush an egg over it, and bake an hour and a half.

Cold lamb makes a very nice pie.

Veal Croquettes.—Remove the gristle, skin, and sinews from a pound of cold veal; mince it finely with four ounces of cold boiled beef or calf's tongue; season with salt, pepper, and nutmeg. Put into a saucepan an ounce of butter rolled in flour, a wineglassful of cream; add the minced meat, and stir for twenty minutes over a slow fire. (If too dry moisten with stock.) Turn the preparation upon a round pie-board; spread it to a smooth layer about an inch thick, and set it in the ice-box to get cold and stiff. It must then be divided into about two dozen pieces, each piece rolled into the form of a cork or round ball over bread-crumbs, then dipped in beaten egg and again rolled in crumbs. Handle carefully so as not to break them. Fry in boiling fat.

Fricassee of Veal.—Take two pounds of lean veal free from skin and bone, and cut it into pieces convenient for serving; fry them in melted butter until the flesh is firm without having acquired any color; dredge a tablespoonful of flour upon them, add a little grated lemon-peel, and gradually as much boiling veal-stock as will cover the meat; simmer until tender. Take out the meat and add to the gravy a gill of boiling cream, salt, cayenne, and a pinch of powdered mace. Beat the yolks of two eggs in a bowl; add gradually a little of the sauce (after it has cooled a few minutes), then add it carefully to the remainder. Return the meat to the sauce, and let the saucepan remain near the fire until the eggs are set. Add the juice of half a lemon and serve immediately.

Fricassee of Lamb.—Take a breast of lamb and cut it into pieces about an inch and a half square; season with salt and pepper. Put them into a saucepan, with a quartered onion, three cloves, a bay-leaf, and three ounces of butter. Cover the saucepan closely, and let it steam gently for half an hour, shaking it occasionally to prevent sticking. Add a pint of boiling water; cover closely once more and boil gently for one hour; then strain the sauce and thicken with a tablespoonful of flour (mix the flour smoothly with a little cold water before adding it to the sauce), boil a moment longer, and serve.

A tablespoonful of very small A. G. capers may be added before serving.

Breast of Lamb with Asparagus Tops.—Remove the skin and part of the fat from a breast of lamb, and cut it into neat pieces; dredge a little flour over them, and place them in a stew-pan with an ounce of butter; let them remain until nicely browned; cover the meat with warm water, add a bunch of parsley, two button onions; simmer until the meat is cooked; skim off the fat, take out the onions and parsley, and mince the latter finely; return it to the gravy with a pint of the tops of boiled asparagus, add salt and pepper, simmer a few minutes longer, and serve. Canned asparagus may be used when the fresh vegetable is out of season.

Fricassee of Chicken.—Take the remains of a cold chicken, cut it into joints, make a gravy by simmering the trimmings in stock enough to cover them, with one onion, stock with three cloves, a bouquet of herbs, salt and pepper. Simmer the gravy for one hour; strain and thicken a cupful of it with a teaspoonful of flour; let this boil, then put in the chicken. Draw the sauce-pan from the fire a few minutes, mix a little of the sauce with the beaten yolks of two eggs and a cupful of cream. Add this last mixture to the saucepan, let it get hot, but on no account allow it to boil, or the eggs will curdle. Serve with the sauce poured over the chicken, and sprinkle a little chopped parsley on top.

Fried Chicken.—Take the remains of a cold chicken, place it in a pan, and simmer with an ounce of butter, a finely-chopped onion, the juice of a lemon, salt and pepper; let them simmer nearly half an hour; take the pieces out and dredge them in flour, and fry in boiling fat; turn the pieces over while cooking, and fry a deep brown.

Make a dressing of flour, mixed smoothly in a cupful of cold milk and a little chopped parsley. Add to the pan that the chicken simmered in, boil gently, strain over the chicken and serve.

Chicken with Rice a la Maryland.—Cut up a chicken into joints, and put it into a stew-pan with the heart, gizzard, and liver, and a slice or two of bacon; cover with warm water, and boil gently until the chicken is quite tender; then take the meat out of the stew-pan, and set it where it will be kept warm; wash half a pint of rice, add it to the gravy, season highly with salt and pepper. When done place the rice upon a dish, lay the chicken on top, and if too dry brush a little melted butter over it.

Chicken Croquettes.—Pound the white meat of a cold chicken with a cold boiled sweetbread in a mortar; add a little salt, beat up an egg with a teaspoonful of flour and a wineglassful of cream; mix the pounded meat with the batter, put it in a sauce-pan, and simmer long enough to absorb the moisture, *stirring all the time;* then turn it into a flat dish, and set it in the ice-box to get cold and stiff, roll it into balls or cones, dip in egg-batter, then roll them in crumbs or cracker-dust and fry in boiling fat.

Chicken a l'Italienne.—Take half a pound of La Favorita macaroni, and boil it in water with a lump of butter. When it has boiled a quarter of an hour, drain off the water and cover the macaroni with milk; add salt and pepper and a whole onion, stock with a few cloves; boil until the macaroni is tender but unbroken.

Boil a chicken in the usual manner, cut it up and lay it on a hot dish, pour the macaroni over it (remove the onion), grate a quarter of a pound of Parmesan cheese over the dish, and brown it in the oven or with a salamander.

Chicken Patties.—Pick the meat from a cold chicken, and cut it up into small dice; place it in a sauce-pan with a cupful of chicken stock, a cupful of cream, a piece of butter the size of an egg, rolled in flour, salt and pepper, and a little grated nutmeg and lemon-peel; simmer gently until it begins to thicken, remove the dish from the fire a few minutes to cool; beat up the yolks of two eggs with a half teaspoonful flour, moistened in milk or cream, and add to the sauce-pan, mix thoroughly, and draw towards the fire (but do not let it boil) until it thickens; before serving add the juice of half a lemon.

Fill your patty-shells with the mixture, one for each person, and serve (see Oyster Patties for patty-shells).

Chicken Pie.—Line the sides of a pie-dish with a good puff paste. Have your chicken cooked as for a fricassee, seasoned with salt and pepper and a little chopped parsley. When they are nearly cooked lay them in a pie-dish with half a pound of salt pork cut into inch squares, and some of the paste cut into inch and a half pieces; pour in a part of the chicken gravy, thicken with a little flour, and cover the dish with the paste cover. Cut a hole the size of a dollar in the cover, and cover it with a piece of dough twice the size of the hole (when baked remove this piece occasionally and examine the interior), brush egg over the pie, and bake in a quick oven.

Should the pie become dry pour in more of the gravy. Pigeon Pie may be made by the above recipe.

Chicken Panada (Invalid cookery).—Take a fresh young chicken and boil it until quite tender, in sufficient water to cover it. Strip the meat from the bones and pound in a mortar until quite smooth, with a little of the liquor it was boiled in; add salt, nutmeg, and a very little grated lemon-peel. Boil this gently for a few minutes, with sufficient liquid to make it the consistency of custard.

Chicken with Dumplings.—Disjoint one chicken, and put to boil in cold water until done. Make dumplings with one pint of flour, one teaspoonful of yeast-powder, and same quantity of salt. Wet this mixture with milk and put with chicken until boiled. Take them out and fry in hot fat until brown; do same with chicken afterwards. Use water in which chicken was boiled to make gravy.

M. G. H.

Chicken Toast.—Take the remains of a cold chicken and chop up fine, put in a sauce-pan, season with salt and pepper and just a little onion, with a lump of butter; break over the meat two or three raw eggs; stir all together, pour it upon nicely-buttered toast, and serve.

Chicken Liver en Brochette.—Wash the livers in cold water, dry them on a towel, and cut them in two; cut slices of bacon into pieces about the same size, and put them on a skewer alternately, and broil. When done brush over them a sauce of melted butter, lemon-juice, pepper and salt.

Braise of Duck with Turnips.—Prepare a domestic duck as for roasting. Line a small pan, just large enough for the duck, with slices of bacon; strew over the bottom a little parsley, powdered herbs, and lemon-peel; lay in the duck, and add a carrot cut into strips, an onion stock with a few cloves, and a dozen whole peppers; cover with stock and add a table spoonful of strong vinegar; baste frequently and simmer until done. Fry some slices of turnip in butter to a light brown, drain and add them to the stew-pan after removing the duck, which should be kept hot. When the turnips are tender remove them, strain the gravy, thickening if necessary with a little flour or arrowroot; put the duck on a dish, throw the hot gravy over it, and garnish with the turnips.

Braise of Duck with Peas.—Prepare and cook a duck as in the above receipt, using green peas instead of carrots and onion, and fry two onions in butter till they are of a pale brown; boil them to a thick sauce with some of the duck gravy; season with salt and pepper, and serve with the peas around the duck and the gravy thrown over.

Salmi of Wild Duck.—Cut up the remains of two roast, underdone wild ducks into neat pieces and set them aside. Take the bones, giblets, and ragged pieces, and put them in a stew-pan with a minced onion or shallot, a saltspoonful salt; and a very little Cayenne; add a pint of stock and a glass of port wine, boil gently half an hour, strain and thicken the sauce with a teaspoonful of prepared brown flour. Put the pieces of duck in a stew-pan, pour the sauce over them, and simmer until quite hot. Add the juice of a sour orange to the dish and serve. A garnish of olives is considered an improvement by some. Soak the olives in cold water one hour; remove the stones with a small vegetable-cutter and add them to the sauce, before taking the dish from the fire.

Salmi of Partridge, Hunter's Style.—Take two cold roast partridges, cut them into joints, and lay them in a saucepan with two ounces of butter, a gill of Bordeaux or port, the grated rind and juice of a large lemon, salt, and a little Cayenne; thicken with a little flour if desired; simmer gently until very hot and serve.

Venison Epicurean.—Cut a steak from the leg or a chop from the loin of venison, about an inch and a half thick. Put a walnut of butter, salt and pepper, into a chafing-dish; light the spirit-lamp under it, and when the butter melts put in the chop or steak; let it cook on one side a few minutes, then turn it over, and add a wineglassful of sherry or port and a tablespoonful of currant-jelly. Simmer gently about seven minutes if it is to be eaten rare, and allow twelve minutes cooking if required well done.

Hot plates and a glass of Mr. Clair's old East India Madeira are all that is requisite to make the feast Apician in character.

Venison Chops, broiled and served with currant-jelly, are not to be despised. Trim the ends as you would a French lamb-chop.

Breast of Venison may be dressed according to the receipt given for breast of mutton.

Venison Patties.—Make a nicely-flavored mince of the remains of cold roast venison; moisten it with a little sherry or gravy, and warm it in a saucepan; fill the patty-shells with the meat and serve. (See oyster patty for patty-shells.)

Broiled Tripe.—Cut up honeycomb tripe into pieces of three to four inches wide; rub a little oil or melted butter over them, dredge them in flour, and broil over a charcoal fire; squeeze a little lemon-juice over each piece, and serve.

Never broil tripe over a hard-coal fire; the gases arising from the coal spoil the flavor of the tripe, making it indigestible and unpalatable.

Tripe Lyonnaise.—Take a pound of cold boiled tripe and cut it into pieces an inch square. Dissolve two ounces of butter in a frying-pan, add a sliced onion to it, and fry until it is tender. Put the pieces of tripe with the onion, a tablespoonful of chopped parsley, a tablespoonful of vinegar, salt, and a little cayenne; heat all gently together. Cover the bottom of a platter with tomato-sauce, add the tripe and serve.

Tripe Fricassee.—Cut up the tripe into square pieces; put them into a stew-pan with a blade of mace, a bouquet of herbs, an onion quartered, salt, and cayenne. Cover the tripe with Rhine wine or water and a little vinegar; stew for one hour. Strain the sauce; put the tripe and sauce in a clean saucepan, with a walnut of butter rolled in flour, a gill of cream, a tablespoonful chopped parsley. Simmer ten minutes, squeeze in the juice of a lemon, and serve.

Pork and Beans.—Wash a quart of beans thoroughly; cover them with cold water and let them soak over-night. Change the water in the morning once or twice. Then put them in a pot and simmer slowly for three hours until they begin to crack open; pour them into a colander to drain off all the water. Heat an earthen bean-pot with hot water, and wipe it dry; place a small piece of pork on the bottom of the pot and pour in the beans. Cut the rind of another piece of pork into strips, and sink it into the beans, leaving only the rind of the pork exposed at the top. Dissolve a tablespoonful of New Orleans molasses, with a teaspoonful of salt, in a pint of warm water, and add it to the pot; set it in the oven and bake slowly for three or four hours, or place the pot in a baker's oven over-night, instructing the baker to add a little water to the pot should the beans become dry.

Serve with Boston brown bread.

Baked Macaroni.—For a small dish one-half pound macaroni, boiled until soft, with a little salt in the water. Drain through a colander; then put in the baking-dish, with one pint and a half of milk, a lump of butter, pepper and salt, and grated cheese (enough to suit taste), and distribute over top. Bake in a hot oven until brown. M. G. H.

Rice Croquettes.—Put a quarter of a pound of Carolina "head" rice, one pint of milk, three tablespoonfuls of powdered sugar, a walnut of butter, and a teaspoonful of *best* extract of vanilla into a saucepan; simmer gently until the rice is tender and the milk absorbed. It must be boiled until thick and dry, or it will be difficult to mould it into croquettes. Beat it thoroughly for three or four minutes; turn it out on a flat tin, and when cold and stiff form it into balls or cones; dip these in beaten egg, roll lightly in crumbs, and fry in hot fat or butter.

VEGETABLE ENTREES.

Stuffed Tomatoes.—Take six ripe tomatoes of equal size; cut off the tops and scoop out the insides; press the pulp through a sieve and mix with it a little salt and cayenne, two ounces of butter broken into little pieces, and two heaping tablespoonfuls of bread-crumbs; fill the tomatoes with the mixture, and bake in a moderate oven. Before serving them brown the stuffing by holding a salamander or a small shovel containing hot coals over them.

Any good force-meat may be used to stuff tomatoes; the remains of game or poultry minced, and mixed with herbs and bread-crumbs, seasoned and bound together with yolk of egg, will suit the most fastidious.

Stuffed Egg-Plant.—Cut the egg-plant in two; scrape out all the inside and put it in a saucepan with a little minced ham; cover with water and boil until soft; drain off the water; add two tablespoonfuls grated crumbs, tablespoonful butter, half a minced onion, salt, and pepper; stuff each half of the hull with the mixture; add a small lump of butter to each and bake fifteen minutes.

Stuffed Egg-Plant, No. 2.—Pare off the purple rind of the egg-plant and quarter it; round off the edges as neatly as possible, then place them in salt and water for an hour. Take them out of the water, scrape out the centre, and mix it with a force-meat of veal, bread-crumbs, seasoning, and yolk of egg; put the mixture in the hollow egg-plant, with a lump of butter upon the top of each, and bake a light brown.

Stuffed Potatoes.—Take a number of firm-skin potatoes of equal size; clean them well and bake them. When done cut off a piece of the end of each potato and scoop out as much of the inside as can be obtained without injury to the skin; mash it with cream and butter; add a little salt; set the dish on the range to keep hot. Take the whites of three eggs, whip them to a froth, and add to the potatoes; mix all together; simmer until quite hot; fill up the skins with the potato paste; fasten the covers with white of egg, and bake fifteen minutes.

Potato Balls.—Boil a small potful of potatoes; wash them well, and mix with them butter, salt, chopped parsley or chives, grated nutmeg, and two raw eggs; work the paste into small balls, dip in beaten egg, roll in cracker-dust or flour, and fry.

Potato Cake.—Take half a pound of dry mealy potatoes, either baked or boiled; mash them until they are free from lumps; mix with them three ounces of flour, salt and pepper, and as much lukewarm milk and butter as will make a smooth, firm dough; add one egg and half a teaspoonful of Royal Baking Powder. Roll the paste out with a rolling-pin till it is nearly two inches thick; dredge a little flour over it, and cut it out the exact size of the frying-pan. Rub the pan over with butter; lay the cake carefully into it; cover with a plate; shake it every now and then to prevent it burning; when it is half done on one side turn it over carefully on the other. Serve on a hot dish with plenty of good fresh butter.

Cold potatoes, if dry and mealy, may be warmed up in this manner.

Sweet potatoes make very good potato cake.

Potato Fritters.—Burst open four nicely-baked potatoes; scoop out the insides with a spoon, and mix with them a wineglassful of cream, a tablespoonful of brandy, two tablespoonfuls of powdered sugar, the juice of one lemon, half a teaspoonful of Thurber's best extract vanilla, and the well-beaten yolks of four and the whites of three eggs; beat the batter for several minutes until it is quite smooth, and drop large tablespoonfuls of the mixture into boiling fat, and fry a light brown; dust powdered sugar over them, and send to table.

Parsnip Fritters.—Boil four good-sized parsnips in salted water until tender; drain them, beat them to a pulp, and squeeze the water from them as much as possible; bind them together with a beaten egg and a little flour. Shape them into cakes, and fry in hot fat.

Oyster-Plant Croquettes.—Wash, scrape, and boil the oyster-plant till tender; rub it through a colander, and mix with the pulp a little butter, cream, salt, cayenne, and lemon-juice; mix the ingredients thoroughly together to a smooth paste, and set the dish in the icebox to get cold; then shape it into small cones, dip them in beaten egg and roll in crumbs, and fry crisp and brown.

Fritters.—The following receipt will serve for many kinds of fruit or vegetable fritters: Make a batter of ten ounces of flour, half a pint of milk, and two ounces of butter; sweeten and flavor to taste; add a glass of brandy, rum, or sherry; stir in the whites of two eggs well beaten; dip the fruit in the batter, and fry. Small fruit and vegetables should be mixed with the batter.

Arrowroot for Batters and Sauces.—Arrowroot may be used to thicken batters, sauces, etc., for those who object to butter, as invalids very often do. Mix a tablespoonful of Beatty's Bermuda Arrowroot smoothly with a little cold water, and stir it into a pint of the batter or sauce.

Omelettes.—Numerous kinds of omelettes may be served as the last entrée, and, if properly made, they generally give satisfaction. As a rule an omelette is a wholesome, inexpensive dish, but yet one in the preparation of which cooks frequently fail owing to ignorance of detail. The flavoring and the ingredients used may be varied indefinitely, but the process is always the same. In making an omelette care should be taken that the frying-pan is hot and dry. The best way to ensure this is to put a small quantity of fat into the pan, let it simmer a few minutes, then pour it out; wipe the pan dry with a towel and put in a little fresh fat, in which the omelette should be fried; care should be taken that the fat does not burn, thereby spoiling the color of the omelette.

It is better to make two or three small omelettes than one large one. The eggs should be but slightly beaten, just long enough to mix them, and no more; a tablespoonful of cream to every two eggs will be found an improvement. Salt *mixed* with the eggs prevents them from rising and gives the omelette a flabby appearance; without salt your omelette will taste insipid; sprinkle a little salt on the omelette just before turning out on the dish.

Oyster Omelette.—Stew six oysters in their own liquor; remove the oysters and thicken the liquid with butter rolled in flour; season with salt, cayenne, and mix with it a teaspoonful chopped parsley. Chop up the oysters and add them to the sauce; simmer gently until the sauce thickens. Beat three eggs lightly with a tablespoonful and a half of cream, and fry until they are delicately set; before folding over put a few spoonfuls of the mixture in the centre; turn it out carefully on a hot dish, with the balance of the sauce round it, and serve immediately.

If small oysters are used put them in the centre of the omelette, whole, fold and serve with sauce round it.

Rum Omelette.—Fry an omelette in the usual way; fold it with a little salt, and turn it out on a hot dish; dust sugar over it, and singe the sugar into stripes with a hot iron rod; pour a wineglassful of warm rum round the omelette, set a light to it, and send to table flaming.

Omelette Souffle.—Break six eggs into separate cups; beat four of the yolks, and mix with them a teaspoonful of flour, three tablespoonfuls of powdered sugar, very little salt, and any flavoring extract that may be preferred. Whisk the white of the six eggs to a firm froth; mix them lightly with the yolks; pour the mixture into a greased pan or dish, and bake in a quick oven. When it is well risen and lightly browned on the top it is done; take it out of the oven, dust a little powdered sugar over it carefully, and send to table immediately. It must be served in the same dish in which it is baked.

Welsh Rarebit.—Select the richest and best American factory cheese—the milder it is the better, as the melting brings out the strength. To make five rarebits take one pound of cheese, grate it, and put it in a tin or porcelain-lined saucepan; add ale enough to thin the cheese sufficiently, say about a wineglassful to each rarebit; stir until all is melted. Have a slice of toast ready for each rarebit (crusts trimmed); put a slice on each plate, and pour cheese enough over each piece to cover it. Eat while hot.

To make a "Golden Buck."—A "Golden Buck" is merely the addition of a poached egg, which is put carefully on the top of the rarebit.

"Yorkshire Rarebit."—This is the same as a "Golden Buck," only it has two thin slices of broiled bacon on the top. —*George Browne, in Thurber's Epicure.*

[See Vegetables, page 90.]

ROASTING.

Roasting is an excellent method of rendering food wholesome and nourishing. Without making any great change in the chemical properties of meat it renders it more tender and highly flavored, while there is not so much waste of its nutritive juices as in baking. But where can the average American get a slice of *roast* beef? Our homes are not provided with spits, bottle-jacks, Dutch ovens, and the like; and as a very sensible writer in the New York *Times* stated, "ninety-nine *roasts* in the United States are baked in ovens, and there is no help for it." I can see no possible way out of the dilemma but to submit gracefully to baked meats for ever. The leading hotels and restaurants overcome the difficulty by purchasing the very best of beef, and keeping it from eight to fifteen days in their ice-houses. Thus the excellent quality of the beef overcomes, in a measure, the bad effects created by the superheated volatile portions that escape from the beef during the process of baking.

No finer, better, or sweeter piece of meat was ever tasted, either in England or America, than the Astor House roast beef; and the secret is in securing the best quality, and taking proper care of it before submitting it to the oven.

Roast Beef.—The best roasting-pieces are the fore and middle ribs and the sirloin. The chuck-ribs, although cheaper, are not as profitable to families, there being too much waste in the carving of them. The ends of the ribs should be removed from the flank, and the latter folded under the beef and securely fastened with skewers. Rub a little salt into the fat part; place the meat in the dripping-pan with a pint of stock or water; baste freely, and dredge with flour half an hour before taking the joint from the oven.

Should the oven be very hot place a buttered paper over the meat to prevent it scorching while yet raw, in which case it will need very little basting; or turn the rib side up towards the fire for the first twenty minutes. The time it will take in cooking depends entirely upon the thickness of the joint and the length of time it has been killed. Skim the fat from the gravy and add a tablespoonful of prepared brown flour and a glass of sherry to the remainder.

Roast Loin of Veal.—Make an incision in the flank or skirt of the loin of veal, and into the cavity thus made, just over the end of the bone, put a well-flavored veal force-meat. Roll in the flank to cover the kidney-fat, and bind it firmly with string or tape. Place a few small veal bones with a few assorted vegetables, cut up, in a dripping-pan; put the loin upon this bed, add half a pint of stock or water, and set it in the oven for twenty minutes; in the meantime work together a tablespoonful of flour with two tablespoonfuls of melted butter; draw the joint from the oven, baste it with the flour and butter, return it to the oven again, and baste occasionally until done.

Veal should be thoroughly done. When it is under-done it is decidedly indigestible and should be avoided.

The breast of veal boned, with a layer of force-meat spread over the inside and rolled and tightly bound, may be substituted for loin of veal.

Mutton.—The choicest mutton in the United States comes from the mountainous regions of Pennsylvania. The animals are semi-domestic and almost as shy and as timid as a deer. In 1878 Col. Duffy, one of Pennsylvania's fish commissioners, dined a party of English gentlemen on mountain-mutton, and they pronounced it the finest-flavored morsel of *venison* they had ever eaten.

Roast Leg of Mutton.—Take a leg of well-kept mutton, rub it lightly with salt, and put it in a dripping-pan with a very little water; cut a potato in two lengthwise, and set it under the leg; baste with a little good dripping at first, and when within twenty minutes of being done, dredge it with flour to get it frothed. Turn the joint two or three times while cooking. Time, about a quarter of an hour to the pound.

Loin of Mutton.—Follow the directions given for roast leg of mutton, but trim off all unnecessary fat, cover the joint with paper until within twenty minutes of its being done, then remove, baste, and flour slightly; serve with currant-jelly. If properly cooked and served *hot* it is a royal dish, but if the fat is not turned to account, a very expensive one.

Lamb.—Put a four or five pound joint of lamb in a dripping-pan with a gill of stock or water; salt and pepper; roll two ounces of butter in a very little flour, divide it into small pieces, and add it here and there upon the meat; set the pan in a moderate oven, and baste frequently until done.

Skim the fat from the gravy, and serve with the lamb; or serve mint-sauce with the joint.

Mint Sauce.—Wash the sprigs of mint, let them dry on a towel, strip off the leaves, and chop them very fine; put in a sauce-boat with a cupful of vinegar and four lumps of sugar; let it stand an hour, and before serving stir all together. Mint sauce, if bottled, will keep for some time, and be just as good, if not better, than it was the first day.

Saddle of Lamb.—A saddle of lamb is a dainty joint for a small party. Sprinkle a little salt over it, and set it in the dripping-pan, with a few small pieces of butter on the meat; baste it occasionally with tried-out lamb-fat; dredge a little flour over it a few minutes before taking from the oven. Serve with the very best of currant-jelly, and send to table with it a few choice early vegetables. Mint-sauce may be served with the joint, but in a very mild form.

Pork.—Pork, more than any other meat, requires to be chosen with the greatest care. The pig, from its gluttonous habits, is particularly liable to disease; and if killed and eaten when in an unhealthy condition, those who partake of it will probably pay dearly for their indulgence. Dairy-fed pork is the best; and knowing this fact, a number of our first-class hotels raise their own pork on farms connected with their country residences. Among them may be mentioned the Continental Hotel, Philadelphia; the Astor, Union Square, Sturtevant, Hoffman, Fifth Avenue, Windsor, and several other leading hotels in New York City. We are indebted to Chas. Lamb for the history of roast pig. In his essays he says: "The art of roasting, or rather broiling (which I take to be the elder brother), was accidentally discovered in the manner following: The swineherd Ho-ti, having gone out into the woods one morning, as his manner was, to collect mast for his hogs, left his cottage in the care of his eldest son, Bo bo, a great, lubberly boy, who, being fond of playing with fire, let some sparks escape into a bundle of straw, which, kindling quickly, spread the conflagration over every part of their poor mansion till it was reduced to ashes. Together with the cottage, what was of much more importance, a fine litter of new farrowed pigs, no less than nine in number, perished. Bo bo was in the utmost consternation, as you may think, not so much for the sake of the tenement—which his father and he could easily build up again with a few dry branches, and the labor of an hour or two, at any time—as for the loss of the pigs. While he was thinking what he should say to his father, and wringing his hands, an odor assailed his nostrils unlike any scent which he had before experienced. What could it proceed from? Not from the burnt cottage; he had smelt that before. Indeed, this was by no means the first accident which had oc-

curred through the negligence of this unlucky firebrand.
A premonitory moistening at the same time overflowed his
nether lip. He knew not what to think. He next stooped down
to feel the pig, if there were any signs of life in it. He burnt
his fingers, and to cool them he applied them in his booby
fashion to his mouth. Some of the crumbs of the scorched
skin had come away with his fingers, and for the first time
in his life (in the world's, indeed, for before him no man
had known it) he tasted—*crackling!* Again he felt and
fumbled at the pig. It did not burn him so much now;
still, he licked his fingers from a sort of habit. The truth
at length broke into his slow understanding that it was the
pig that smelt so and the pig that tasted so delicious; and
surrendering himself up to the new-born pleasure, he fell to
tearing up whole handfuls of the scorched skin, with the
flesh next it, and was cramming it down his throat in his
beastly fashion when his sire entered amid the smoking
rafters, and, finding how affairs stood, began to rain blows
upon the young rogue's shoulders as thick as hailstones,
which Bo-bo heeded not any more than if they had been
flies. The tickling pleasure which he experienced in his lower
regions had rendered him quite callous to any inconveniences
he might feel in those remote quarters. Bo-bo's scent, being wonderfully sharpened since morning, soon raked out
another pig, and, fairly rending it asunder, thrust the
lesser half by main force into the fists of Ho-ti, still shout-
ing out, 'Eat, eat! Eat the burnt pig, father! Only taste!'
It is needless to state that both father and son despatched
the remainder of the litter. Bo-bo was strictly enjoined not
to let the secret escape. Nevertheless strange stories got
about; it was observed that Ho-ti's cottage was burnt down
now more frequently than ever. As often as the sow farrowed, so soon was the house of Ho-ti seen to be in a blaze.
At length they were watched, the terrible mystery discovered,
and father and son summoned to take their trial at Peking,
then an inconsiderable assize town. Evidence was given,
the obnoxious food itself produced in court, and verdict
about to be pronounced, when the foreman of the jury

begged that some of the burnt pig of which the culprit stood accused might be handed into the box. He handled it, and they all handled it; and burning their fingers as Bo-bo and his father had done before them, and nature prompting to each of them the same remedy, against the face of all the facts and the clearest charge which judge had ever given, to the surprise of the whole court, townsfolk, strangers, reporters (they had Howards and Raymonds in those days), and all present, without leaving the box, or any manner of consultation whatever, they brought in a simultaneous verdict of not guilty."

Dr. Kitchiner on Pork.—"Take particular care it be done enough. Other meats underdone are unpleasant, but pork is absolutely uneatable; the sight of it is enough to appall the sharpest appetite, if its gravy has the least tint of redness. Be careful of the crackling; if this be not crisp, or if it be burned, you will be scolded."

The Turkey.—The turkey, says Brillat-Savarin, "is the largest, and, if not the most delicate, at least the most savory of domestic poultry. It enjoys the singular advantage of assembling around it every class of society. When our farmers and wine-growers regale themselves on a winter's evening, what do we see roasting before the kitchen fire, close to which the white-clothed table is set? A turkey! When the useful tradesman or the hard-worked artist invites a few friends to an occasional treat, what dish is he expected to set before them? A nice roast turkey stuffed with sausage-meat and Lyons chestnuts. And in our highest gastronomical society, when politics are obliged to give way to dissertations on matters of taste, what is desired, what is awaited, what is looked out for at the second course? A truffled turkey. In my 'Secret Memoirs' I find sundry notes recording that on many occasions its restorative juice has illumined diplomatic faces of the highest eminence."

Now, the average American could not be induced to eat a turkey stuffed with sausage-meat; he would naturally say that if the useful tradesman "or the hard-working artist" experienced any pleasure over such a compound, he was welcome to it; to him sausage-meat was too suggestive of pork and—mystery. But the Lyons chestnuts—ah! yes, that will do, for he has tasted chestnut stuffing and has learned to like it. A dissertation on truffles, while waiting for the "truffled turkey" to be served, is all that is necessary to make him say he is passionately fond of them in any form, otherwise he would be apt to ask the waiter to remove the dressing from his plate, "as it was full of small pieces of charcoal" (an actual occurrence).

Roast Turkey.—Singe the bird, and in drawing it preserve the heart, gizzard, and liver; remove the gall-bag from the liver, and be very careful not to break it, as if any of the liquid touches the bird no amount of washing will remove the bitter taste. Cut off the neck close to the body, and before doing so push back the skin of the neck so that sufficient may be left on to turn over the back; remove a part of the fat adhering to the skin; split the breast-bone from the inside, or place several folds of cloth on the high breast-bone and break and flatten it a little with a rolling-pin to make the bird look plump. Fill the breast and body with stuffing; sew up the opening with coarse thread; turn the neck-skin over the back and fasten it; truss the legs close to the breast, the wings turn over the back, using skewers or twine to hold them in proper position. Put the turkey in the dripping-pan with a little hot water, dredge it with flour, and lay a few small pieces of butter upon it, and the feet, scalded and scraped, under it. Baste frequently. Time, from two to three hours, according to the size of the bird.

Should he prove to be of doubtful age and rich in spurs and scaly feet, parboil him. Put him in a saucepan or pot, cover with cold water, add a teaspoonful of salt, and when the water comes to a boil take out the bird and dry it well before stuffing it.

Chestnut Stuffing.—Roast a pint of chestnuts and peel off the outer and inner skin; weigh them, and simmer half a pound of them for twenty minutes in as much veal gravy as will cover them; drain and let them cool; then pound them in a mortar with four ounces of butter, three ounces of bread-crumbs, a trifle of grated lemon-peel and powdered mace, salt, and a pinch of cayenne; bind the mixture with the yolks of three eggs.

Chestnuts roasted or boiled may be added to almost any stuffing for fowl, etc., and give general satisfaction. I once made a stuffing of chestnuts, apple-sauce, bread-crumbs, and the proper seasoning for a 'possum, and all who tasted of it pronounced it a dainty dish. One of the party, Dr. H——, never tires of talking about "that 'possum with the chestnuts."

Oyster Stuffing.—Remove the heart (or what some call the eye) from two dozen oysters, mince them finely, pound them to a paste, and mix with them five ounces of bread-crumbs, an ounce of butter, the grated rind of half a lemon, a tablespoonful of chopped parsley, a pinch of cayenne, an even teaspoonful of salt, and half a teaspoonful of pepper. When well mixed bind the mixture with the yolk of an egg and a small quantity of the oyster liquid added gradually.

Bread Stuffing.—Grate sufficient bread to fill the bird; moisten it with milk, and season with salt, pepper, sweet marjoram, and the grated rind of one lemon. Add a tablespoonful of butter, and bind the mixture with yolk of egg. Add a few raw whole oysters, if desired.

Roast Capon.—They should be managed in the same way as turkeys, and served with the same sauces. I cannot quite come to the conclusion that a roast capon is equal in flavor to one boiled and served with egg-sauce.

Roast Chicken.—Singe your chickens and truss them carefully. Broilers, as they are called, are better without stuffing, unless they are very large. Season with salt, put small bits of butter over the meat, and place them in the pan with a little water or veal stock; baste occasionally and dredge with flour before taking from the oven. A few tarragon leaves with the sauce are acceptable.

A spring chicken cooked in any style is not to be despised by any means, but I quite agree with that appreciative epicure, Mr. Sam Ward, when he said:

> "To roast spring chickens is to spoil 'em;
> Just split 'em down the back and broil 'em."

Roast Pigeon.—Raise the skin from the breast-bones of the pigeons with your finger; make a small quantity of finely-flavored stuffing, and stuff it between the skin and flesh, using care not to break the skin. Fasten a long, thin slice of bacon over the breasts of the birds with toothpicks; put them in a dripping-pan with a little water, and dredge with flour. When done remove the bacon, set them neatly around the edge of a dish, fill the centre with new green peas or Godillot French peas, and serve. (A favorite dish of the members of the Club of Lindenthorpe, on the Delaware.)

Roast Domestic Duck.—Americans, as a rule, do not take kindly to domestic duck, owing to its peculiar flavor and richness, and also to the fact of the bird being usually accompanied with a very highly-seasoned onion stuffing. Nevertheless, a young domestic duck stuffed with a bread stuffing seasoned with salt, pepper, sage, and a *suspicion* of onion, is a dish that should often appear upon the tables of our American families. A pair of ducklings with no other stuffing than an onion placed inside the birds while roasting, and removed before serving, will make a splendid dinner for a family of five or six. Serve with apple-fritters or apple-sauce.

Roast Goose.—Singe, draw, and truss the goose, and, if an old one, parboil it. The best stuffing for a goose is a sage-and-onion stuffing. The way in which this is made must depend upon the taste of those who have to eat it. If a strong flavor of onions is liked the onion should be chopped raw. If this is not the case they should be boiled in one or two waters, and mixed with bread-crumbs, powdered sage, salt and pepper, nutmeg, and two small apples chopped fine; fill the bird with the stuffing, sew it up with coarse thread, sprinkle salt over it, and set it in a pan with a little warm water; baste frequently, and do not take it from the oven until thoroughly cooked.

Ham a la Russe.—If the ham be hard and salty soak it for several hours. If a fresh-cured Ferris ham it will not need soaking. Trim and cut away all the rusty parts, and cover it with a coarse paste of flour and water half an inch thick, and fasten it securely to prevent the juice escaping. Time, from three to four hours, according to size of the ham. Remove the paste and skin while the ham is hot, cover the fat with a sugar paste (see boiled ham) moistened with port, and return it to the oven a few minutes to brown.

The Continental Hotel, Philadelphia, makes a specialty of *Ham à la Russe,* and it is a splendid dish served with champagne-sauce.

Canvas-Back Duck.—Pluck, draw, and singe the duck; wipe out the blood from the inside with a clean towel; cut off the head and neck, and put them in the body of the duck, allowing the head to protrude. Sprinkle a little celery-salt over the breast, with a bit of butter; put it on a small buttered pan, and set it in the oven for seventeen minutes. Serve with currant-jelly.

A few outer stalks of celery placed inside the duck will improve its flavor.

A red-head duck stuffed with grated bread, chopped celery, seasoning, and mixed with yolk of egg, will taste very much like a canvas-back.

A blue-winged teal duck is very nice broiled. Cut it down the back, brush a little melted butter over it, and broil, keeping the inner part of the duck to the fire most of the time. To roast a teal place a strip of bacon over the breast and set it in the oven for fifteen minutes.

Roast Venison.—Take a leg of well-kept venison, wipe it thoroughly, rub a little salt over it, and dredge with flour.

Place it in a dripping-pan with the ragged pieces you have trimmed off of it, and a little water or wine. Put small bits of butter here and there over the meat, set it in the oven, and baste frequently till done. If the leg is not very fat it is a good plan to lard it with strips of bacon or pork. Serve with currant-jelly, and don't forget the hot plates.

I am not a lover of venison à l'Anglaise, for I do not fancy the flour paste daubed over the meat as most English cooks prepare it, though the buttered paper is an advantage when cooking large joints of game.

Roast Prairie Chicken.—The bird being a little strong, and its flesh when cooked a little dry, it should be either larded or wide strips of bacon or pork placed over its breast. A mild seasoned stuffing will improve the flavor of old birds. Dust a little flour over them, baste occasionally, and serve.

Pheasants may be managed in the same manner.

Roast Quail.—Pluck and draw the birds, rub a little butter over them, tie a strip of bacon over the breasts, and set them in the oven for twenty to twenty-five minutes.

Roast Woodcock.—Pluck the bird carefully, do not cut off the head or draw the trail; punch a few holes in the back of the bird with a fork, and lay it in the pan on a piece of buttered toast. A little salt is all the seasoning required. Time, twenty minutes. A woodcock is the only game-bird I send to table without currant-jelly; its own fine flavor needs no bush.

Roast Snipe.—Pluck and draw the snipe, preserving the trail and head; tie a thin strip of bacon over the breast; chop up the trail and spread it on buttered toast (one slice for each bird); lay the birds in the pan with the toast between them, and roast twenty minutes. Remove the bacon, place the birds on the toast, and serve.

Rail-Birds.—Rail-birds are decidedly inferior to either snipe or woodcock. They should be skinned, as much of their rankness lies in the skin. The trail is a trifle too strong for the average American palate. They make a very good pie; manage them as you would snipe for roasting, broiling, etc.

Reed-Birds.—These delicious "lumps of sweetness," as they are appropriately called, are always acceptable, but to thoroughly appreciate a reed-bird dinner one must mingle with the gunners on the Delaware River as guest or member of one of the many clubs whose houses are situated within a few hundred yards from the hunting-grounds.

After the judge's decision as to who has *high boat* the birds are plucked (and at some of the club-houses drawn) arranged neatly in a dripping-pan with bits of fresh country butter between them. They are allowed to cook on one side a few minutes, and with a long-handled spoon are turned over to brown the other side. A little salt is added, and they are then placed upon a hot platter *en pyramide* and the gravy poured over them; they are then sent to table with fried chip potatoes. The scene that follows baffles description. Not a voice is heard, "at least as long as the birds last." The painful silence is only broken by the sounds of crumbling bones between the teeth of the assemblage, and an occasional *More birds, Mr. Caterer!* from that prince of gourmets, Mayor S——.

Reed-Birds a la Lindenthorpe.—On "Ladies' Day" the members of this club are more particular than on "members' day." They prepare the birds by drawing the trail and removing the heads; they then take large sweet or Irish potatoes, cut them in two, scoop out the insides, and put an oyster or a small piece of bacon inside of each bird, and put the birds inside the potato, tie them up with twine, and bake until the potatoes are done. The common twine is then removed and the potatoes are tied with a narrow piece of white or colored tape, in a neat bow-knot, and sent to table on a napkin.

SALADS.

There is not a dish in the gastronomic vocabulary that varies in composition more than a salad. And the reasons for it are many. Among them may be mentioned climatic influences and the personal habits of individuals. The individual who lives well, and who considers a meal imperfect without a wine or malt beverage, will sooner or later learn to use condiments to such an extent as to alarm the more temperate at table. A salad prepared for the majority, he will tell you, cloys on his palate; and, after the first mouthful he resorts to cayenne and vinegar to "tone up" the salad to suit his taste. After this ungenerous act the close observer will notice confusion upon the face of the salad-composer, who felt confident that he had prepared a salad to suit the taste of the most fastidious. But my friend the salad-mixer should not get offended; he should keep in view one fact—that a palate abused by the constant use of tobacco and other stimulants requires more sharp and pungent seasoning than one accustomed to these things only in moderation, and that a strictly temperate person requires less of condiments than either of them.

The dyspeptic's case is entirely different. He will complain of a salad in any form, accusing the oil of causing all his trouble. But he is wrong. Let him stop flooding his food with liquids that only dilute and weaken the gastric juices of the stomach and he will soon be rid of dyspepsia and learn to love salads as much as other people. The habit of washing down each mouthful of food with liquids is a deplorable one, and the person that does it invites dyspepsia by so doing. Persons who are in the habit of eating salads late at night, and who complain of indigestion next morning, will find it to their advantage to add half a teaspoonful of chicken pepsin to each pint of Mayonnaise; by so doing digestion is assisted, and everyone will feel very much better next day.

In catering for families I invariably add pepsin to the dressing, but until now have kept it a secret, not liking the idea of being accused of mixing medicine with the food. Nevertheless I have been amply rewarded by receiving more orders than I could personally attend to.

The following letter will explain itself:

SHARPLESS & SONS, 801 to 807 Chestnut St.,
PHILADELPHIA, March 7, 1879.

Mr. Murrey, Continental Hotel:

DEAR SIR: Please send two quarts of chicken salad manipulated by *yourself;* the last we had prepared by you left a pleasant recollection. Send up promptly at five o'clock, and oblige, C. H. HAMRICK.

Lettuce Salad.—Take a good-sized head of lettuce and pull the leaves apart. Wash them a moment in a little water, then shake off the water and dry the leaves in a napkin by taking hold of the four corners and shaking it. Examine them carefully, wipe off all grit, and reject all bruised leaves; place them in a salad-bowl large enough to dress them in nicely without scattering a part of them over the table. Mix one salt-spoonful of salt, one salt-spoonful of fresh ground pepper, and a dust of cayenne with a tablespoonful of oil in a salad-spoon; pour this over the lettuce, and add two more tablespoonfuls of oil; next toss the salad lightly with a salad spoon and fork, and, lastly, add a tablespoonful of vinegar; toss it gently once or twice and send to table. *To be eaten at once.* Never cut lettuce. Should you wish to divide the leaves tear them apart gently. But it is not always necessary to tear the leaves, should they appear too large to eat gracefully. With the assistance of your knife you can wrap the leaf round the end of your fork so as to make a small ball of it, and eat it with a little more elegance than your neighbor, who is trying his level best to get the leaf into his mouth edgeways.

Plain French Dressing.—A plain French dressing is made of salt, pepper, oil, and vinegar, and nothing else. Three tablespoonfuls of oil to one of vinegar, salt-spoon heaping full of salt, an even salt-spoonful of pepper mixed with a little cayenne.

Plain English Dressing.—Same as plain French dressing, with a teaspoonful of made English mustard added.

Bacon Dresing.—Cut half a pound of bacon-fat into slices, then into very small pieces, and fry them until the oil extracted is a light-brown; remove the pan from the fire and add the juice of a lemon, one wineglassful of strong vinegar, a salt-spoonful of pepper, and pour it over the salad with the pieces of bacon. A very nice dressing when you cannot get oil, etc.

Summer Mayonnaise.—Chop up the yolk and white of a hard-boiled egg very fine, and sprinkle it over a salad. Mix a plain French dressing in a cold soup-plate, and pour over the egg and salad, and mix all together.

Sauce Vinaigrette.—Mix a plain French dressing, and add to it a quarter of an onion chopped fine, a teaspoonful of chopped parsley or pickle.

Don't like the onion? Then add a few Godillot capers.

Mayonnaise Sauce.—Work the yolks of two raw eggs to a smooth paste, and add two salt-spoonfuls of Royal Table Salt, half a salt-spoonful of cayenne, a salt-spoonful of dry mustard, and a teaspoonful of oil; mix these ingredients thoroughly and add the strained juice of half a lemon. Take the remainder of half a pint of Virgin olive-oil and add it gradually, a teaspoonful at a time, and every fifth teaspoonful add a few drops of lemon-juice until you have used two lemons and the half-pint of oil.

There are almost as many ways of making a Mayonnaise sauce as there are of cooking eggs.

Mayonnaise Sauce, No. 2.—Rub the yolks of three hard-boiled eggs with the yolk of one raw egg to a smooth paste; add a heaping teaspoonful of salt, two salt-spoonfuls of white pepper, and two salt-spoonfuls of made mustard; mix thoroughly and work a gill of oil gradually into the mixture, alternated with a teaspoonful of tarragon vinegar until you have used three tablespoonfuls of vinegar. Should the sauce appear too thick add a wineglassful of cream gradually.

Lobster Salad.—Tear the meat of the lobster into shreds with two forks ; remove the eggs (*if a hen lobster*) from the fins ; scrape out all the green fat from the shell and set it aside. Prepare for making a Mayonnaise by working a tablespoonful of the fat into a smooth paste ; let this green fat, with the yolk of one raw egg and one hard-boiled egg, be the basis of your Mayonnaise ; in all other particulars follow instruction for Mayonnaise sauce. When complete mix the lobster meat with three tablespoonfuls of the sauce. Cover the bottom of a dish or compot with lettuce (the large leaves tear in two), put a layer of lobster upon it; next add a layer of celery cut into narrow-inch strips, and another layer of lobster ; arrange it neatly on the dish ; sprinkle the eggs or the chopped coral on the lettuce round the edges ; pour the sauce over the meat, garnish with lobster-legs, and serve.

Somebody sent to the Washington *Republic's* correspondent, "G. H. B.," while he was laid up in Providence hospital with the gout, a very fine lobster, and this is what he did with it : " Now, I'll tell you about that lobster. I had him laid away tenderly in the ice-chest, and directed him to appear at dinner with some leaves of lettuce and a raw egg. The yolk of that egg I mingled, with slow, deliberate revolutions of a fork, with mustard, red pepper, salt, and oil. When the paste was thick enough to take up on the end of the fork like dough I thinned it—'cut it' is technical—with vinegar, and there was my dressing. I planted a table facing the snow-storm, at which I mocked and jeered in a temperature of seventy degrees Fahrenheit. Then did I disrobe the 'Cardinal of the Seas' (you remember the Frenchman who applied that to lobsters, thinking they came from the ocean red ?) of his vestments, and by the aid of a long pickle-spoon placed all that was in him on the plate. His legs I chewed up. Then I ate him, and watched the many industrious, hard-working fathers of families trudging by in the snow, who had no lobster, and couldn't have dressed him if they had. Then I finished up on some sponge-cake and custard, ate two apples with a sprinkle of salt, lit my pipe, and in its smoke framed beautiful porcelain figures engraven with

Chinese characters and Hindoo idols. That's what I did with that lobster. He was a prime one and very much interested the Sisters."

Chicken Salad.—Cut up a cold boiled chicken into neat strips or pieces, and mix with it an equal quantity of celery. Cut the celery-stalks into inch pieces, and cut each piece into long strips; mix them together with a few spoonfuls of Mayonnaise; arrange neatly upon a dish garnished with lettuce, parsley, or hard-boiled egg, pour the remainder of the sauce over the meat, and serve.

Veal Salad.—Boil a nice lean piece of veal with a chicken or turkey, saving the water in which they were boiled to make a soup, and serving the fowl for dinner with egg or oyster sauce. When cold cut it up into neat strips, mix it with celery or lettuce, pour Mayonnaise over it, and serve.

The custom of pickling the pieces, etc., of fowl before mixing them in a salad does not take well with Americans.

Herring Salad.—Soak four Holland herrings in water or milk for three hours; then cut them up into neat, square pieces and set them aside; cut up into slices nearly three quarts of boiled potatoes while they are hot, and pour over them Rhine wine enough to moisten them; cover close, and when cold add the herrings and the yolks of four hard-boiled eggs chopped fine; crush a dozen whole peppers in a napkin, add to the salad, and mix. If milt herrings are used pound the milt to a paste, moisten it with vinegar, and pour over the salad.

If roe herring are used, separate the eggs neatly and sprinkle them over the salad, and serve.

I know a number of my German friends who will say, "Ah! that is not a herring salad." Where are the apples, the capers, beets, pickles, etc.? But the only answe I can make them is that the majority of our German brethren make an Italian or a Russian salad and call it a herring salad.

Potato Salad.—Cut up three quarts of boiled potatoes, *while hot*, into neat pieces, and add to them a tablespoonful of chopped parsley, a tablespoonful of chopped onion, a teaspoonful of pepper, and one of salt; add a cupful of oil, and mix; then add a cupful of warm stock, a wineglassful of vinegar (from the mixed-pickle bottle), mix the ingredients together carefully, and do not break the potato any more than is absolutely necessary; set it in the ice-box, and when cold serve by placing a leaf of lettuce on a side-dish, and put two spoonfuls of the salad upon the lettuce. The onion and parsley may be omitted, and boiled root celery added, or a little stalk celery chopped fine. You cannot make a perfect potato salad with cold boiled potatoes. Most cook-books recommend them, but that soggy, peculiar taste cannot be removed or destroyed by all the condiments in the cruet-stand. A salad prepared while the potatoes are hot will look more appetizing and will keep three or four days, while cold boiled potatoes will turn a black, uninviting color, and turn sour the second day.

Turnip Tops.—When turnips placed in the cellar begin to sprout they are usually thrown away, but the housekeeper of experience will tell you that a bushel of turnips will furnish her family with a salad all winter, and a very good one if properly prepared.

Place the bushel of turnips in a dark, warm cellar to sprout, and when the sprouts are three or four inches long cut them off; pick the leaves from the stems, and pour hot water over them; let them remain in the hot water a moment, then plunge them into cold water; place the sprouts in the colander to drain off all the water, and send to table with a plain dressing or bacon dressing poured over them.

Asparagus Salad.—Boil the asparagus, and take it from the hot water and plunge it into cold water to give it firmness; drain off the water, and send to table with sauce Vinaigrette or plain French dressing.

Hop Sprouts.—The hop-growers pull up all but two or three sprouts from a hill of hops, and throw them away; the few that remain in the hill are supposed to do duty as pole-climbers. Gather a small basketful of the rejected sprouts; take them home; boil them in salted water a few minutes, then plunge them into cold water; drain off all the water, and serve with a plain French dressing, bacon dressing, or sauce Vinaigrette.

If you eat asparagus you will like hop sprouts.

Cucumber Salad.—Peel and slice the cucumbers as thin as possible; put the slices in salted water five minutes, then draw off the water; cover them with vinegar, half a teaspoonful of pepper, and salt if necessary.

Cucumber and Tomato Salad.—Peel and slice a five-inch cucumber into very thin slices; put them in a bowl with half a teaspoonful of salt and two tablespoonfuls of vinegar; set it aside and mix a plain English dressing.

Take one large or two small-sized tomatoes, scald them a moment, remove the skin and put them in cold water a few minutes to cool; line the salad-bowl with lettuce, drain the cucumbers from the pickle and put them in the bowl; wipe the tomatoes and cut them into slices; put them on top of the cucumber, pour the dressing over it, and serve.

OFFICE WESTERN UNION TELEGRAPH COMPANY,
HARRISBURG, PENN., April 16, 1879.

Mr. Murrey, Caterer Continental Hotel, Philadelphia:

Send by express, to-morrow, one hundred Murrey salad sandwiches.

HENRY M. HOYT, *Governor.*

Murrey's Salad Sandwich.—Cut up four ounces of breast of boiled chicken and four ounces of tongue, place them in a mortar, and pound them to a paste; add two salt-spoonfuls of celery-salt, a pinch of cayenne, a teaspoonful of anchovy paste, and four tablespoonfuls of Mayonnaise; put the mixture on a cold dish, and set it aside.

Take a few neat leaves of lettuce, dip each leaf in a little tarragon vinegar, shake it, and place it on a slice of bread; spread a layer of the prepared meat over the lettuce, then another leaf of lettuce over the meat, and the other slice of bread, and your sandwich is made. Trim off the crust, cut each sandwich in two, and fold each piece neatly in confectionery (oiled) paper.

Ham and veal make a nice salad sandwich. The meat may be spread on the bread and the lettuce in the centre, if preferred.

Muskmelon Salad.—Should you be so unfortunate as to receive an insipid, over-ripe melon, do not send it from the table, but scoop it out on your plate with a spoon, pour a French dressing over it, and you will thank me for the suggestion.

Alligator-Pear Salad.—This tropical fruit, that tastes something like our chestnuts, is beginning to find favor among us, but care should be used in selecting the fruit. The green colored fruit is the best; the black, over-ripe fruit is useless. Cut the pear in two, remove the large seed, cut away the outer rind, then cut the fruit into strips and season with a salt-spoonful of salt, two tablespoonfuls best Virgin olive-oil, a teaspoonful of tarragon vinegar—nothing else.

Salt.—Of all the condiments now in use salt is the most essential. The health of every individual depends upon it, and it is as much required as food or drink; therefore the salt question is an important one to families. Do not buy salt so fine as to cake in the salt-cellar, for it is almost useless; nor use a very coarse salt; a happy medium is the thing. What is known to the trade as Royal Table Salt is the proper fineness and best adapted for hotels and family use.

Mushrooms.—I have purposely avoided introducing mushrooms into my receipts on account of the expense attached, but where the expense is only a secondary consideration they may be used indiscriminately. Of the French canned mushrooms the A. Godillot's brand gives the best satisfaction, being put up and sealed at the source of supply, and, therefore, their natural flavors are preserved. Our field mushrooms are very nice when fresh, cooked in any form. To distinguish them from the poisonous fungi, "A Constant Reader," writing to the London *Times*, says: "I venture to send you a simple test of the mushroom, which I have practised for many years, and for which I am indebted to an old herbalist. Before peeling the mushroom pass a gold ring backwards and forwards on the skin of the mushroom; should the bruise thus caused turn yellow or orange color the mushroom is poisonous, but otherwise it is quite safe. I have tried repeated baskets of mushrooms in this way, some turning yellow and others retaining the usual color, though in all other respects to all appearance the same."

Forney's *Progress* on mushrooms:

He saw a fellow gathering mushrooms, and he knew they were the poisonous kind.

"Take care," he said, "those mushrooms are poisonous."

"Oh! that makes no difference," replied the man. "I am not going to eat them; I'm gathering them for market."

The Mystery of making Loaf Bread--A Trustworthy Receipt.—"Loaf bread," once said an experienced housekeeper to us, "interferes with the salvation of more housekeepers than any other one thing in the world." This was probably an extravagant statement, yet to the country housewife who cannot turn to a convenient bakery the duty of breadmaking is too often a heavy cross—a sort of hit-or-miss experiment. Heavy, sour bread is far more general than the opposite, and this is trying to both the digestions and to the tempers of the family who eat it. Yet there is no reason for this; there is a philosophy of breadmaking as of everything else, and certain causes accomplish certain results. Therefore we are glad to be able to give a receipt from a practical housekeeper whose bread *never* fails: To make two quarts of bread or rolls take four or five nice, large Irish potatoes, peel and cut them up, and put them to boil in just enough water to cover them. When done mash smooth in the same water, and when *cool*, not *cold*, add a half-teacupful of yeast—or, if you use compressed yeast, the sixth part of a cake dissolved in tepid water—a dessert-spoonful of sugar, a little salt, a tablespoonful of lard, and a pint of flour. Mix together lightly. This should be very soft and quite sticky. Set by in a covered vessel in a warm place to rise. In two or three hours it will be risen, and should look almost like yeast, full of bubbles. Now work in the rest of your two quarts of flour, and, if necessary, add a little cold water. The dough should be rather soft and need not be kneaded more than half an hour. Set to rest in a moderately warm place for four hours or thereabouts. It can be baked now if wanted at once, but, if not, take a spoon and push the dough down from the top and sides of the vessel containing it, and let it rise again. The oftener the bread rises the lighter it will be—three times is, however, sufficient. After it rises the last time take it out of the vessel and knead it with your hands until it is smooth. If too soft add a little more flour. For rolls, roll out and cut as if for biscuit. If you prefer doubled rolls give each a touch with the rolling-pin to make it oblong, and then double it over. The baking-pan must be greased and the rolls must not touch each other. Set down to rise; this will take half or three-quarters of an hour. Then put in the oven and bake as you would biscuit. Unless the oven is *hot* the rolls will spread and the crust be hard.—*Col. McClure's Philadelphia Times.*

Wheat Bread.—Put seven pounds of flour into a bread-pan, hollow out the centre, and add a quart of lukewarm water, a teaspoonful of salt, and a wineglassful of yeast. Have ready more warm water, and add gradually as much as will make a smooth, soft dough. Knead it well; dust a little flour over it, cover it with a cloth, and set it in a warm place for four hours; then knead it again for fifteen minutes and let it rise again. Divide it into loaves and bake in a quick oven.

Corn Bread.—Sift three quarts of corn meal, add a tablespoonful of salt, and mix sufficient water with it to make a very thin batter. Cover it with a bread-cloth and set it to rise. When ready to bake stir it well, pour it into a baking-pan, and bake slowly. Use cold water in summer and hot water in winter.

Continental Hotel Corn Bread.—Sift together a pound and a half wheat flour, one pound Indian meal, two ounces Royal Baking Powder, and a tablespoonful salt. Beat together three ounces of sugar, three ounces of butter, and four eggs; add the mixture to the flour, and make a stiff batter by adding warm milk if in winter, cold milk in summer. Bake in small square moulds.

Continental Hotel Muffins.—Mix two and a half pounds flour, three ounces Royal Baking Powder, and tablespoonful salt. Beat up three ounces of sugar, three ounces butter, and four eggs together ; add to the flour, make a batter with milk, half fill the muffin-rings, and bake in a quick oven.

Boston Brown Bread.—Sift together thoroughly half a pint of flour, one pint corn meal, half a pint rye flour, one teaspoonful salt, one tablespoonful brown sugar, and two teaspoonfuls baking powder. Peel, wash, and boil two mealy potatoes; rub them through the sieve, diluting with half a pint of water. When this is quite cold use it to make a batter and pour it into a well-greased mould having a cover. Place it in a saucepan of boiling water. Simmer one hour without the water getting into it ; take it out of the water, remove the cover, and finish cooking by baking about thirty minutes.

Steamed Brown Bread.—One quart each of milk and Indian meal, one pint of rye meal, one cup of molasses, two teaspoonfuls of soda. Add a little salt and steam four hours.

M. G. H.

Milk Biscuit.—Take one-fourth of a pound butter, one quart lukewarm milk, two wineglassfuls yeast, salt to taste, and as much flour as will form the dough. Stir flour into the milk to make a thick batter, and add the yeast. This should be done in the evening. Next morning melt the butter and pour it into the sponge; add flour enough to make a stiff dough; knead it well and set it aside to rise. When perfectly light roll it out an inch thick and cut the biscuits, set them in shallow baking-pans, and set them in a moderately warm place to rise. When they are light brush beaten egg over them and bake in a quick oven.

Corn Cakes.—Scrape twelve ears of corn, use two eggs, one and one-half cups of milk, salt and pepper to taste, and flour enough to hold all together. Fry in hot fat. M. G. H.

Fried Bread Cakes.—Add half a cupful of melted butter, three of "A" sugar, four eggs, teaspoonful of salt, and a little grated nutmeg to five cupfuls of dough. Knead these well together with flour, and set it before the fire to rise until very light. Knead the dough again after it rises, and cut it into diamond or crescent shaped cakes; let them rise, and fry them in boiling fat.

Pies.—Pie, and the extent to which it is consumed in this country, have long been a subject upon which Europeans travelling here have exercised their descriptive and imaginative powers. It seems to be a cardinal belief on the other side that no meal is furnished here without a superabundance of pie; that, even at the best inns and restaurants in New York, Boston, and Philadelphia, pie is devoured at breakfast, luncheon, dinner, and supper; that no American would sit down to a table where he could not see plenty of pie; that all the States are closely connected and bound together by a prejudice in favor of pie; that it was love of pie rather than force of patriotism which, in the civil war, preserved the Union. Sala is one of the latest Englishmen to descant on the omnipresence and national omnivorousness of pie. He devotes ample space to it in one of his recent letters to the London *Telegraph;* admits that he has eaten it, and that it is so very toothsome that it is difficult to resist its temptations. He has done what a great many of our own people never do. Hundreds of families in this and in other cities do not see a pie from beginning to end of the year. Thousands of natives have never tasted pie. In the large towns of the Middle States it is but seldom put on the table. New England, indeed, is the region to which pie is indigenous, though even there it is confined mainly to the rural districts. It appears odd, however, that Englishmen should so animadvert on our pies, as if they had never tasted or heard of such things. They have any quantity of pies at home, but these are meat pies, commonly of pork and mutton, and as hostile to gastric conditions as bad pastry and poor baking can conveniently make them. They have, too, any number of fruit pies, giving them the name of tarts, not to be compared with our pies. The gooseberry tart, almost as much a British dish as plum-pudding, is eaten from Cornwall to Northumberland, and that its eaters survive it proves the strength and elasticity of the national stomach. It is usually as heavy as lead and a guarantee of indigestion. The French also have numberless pies under the disguise of *tartes*, but no better than, often not so good as, ours. In truth, the American pie is widely prevalent in the Old World, where, as a rule, it is inferior to the native article. *NEW YORK TIMES.*

Puff Paste.—Good sweet, salt butter, which has been washed in cold water, squeezed between the hands to free it from the salt, and afterwards wrung in a cloth to take away all the moisture, is the best material that can be used. The consistency of the butter is of much importance. If it is too hard it will not easily mix with the flour, but if it is too soft the paste will be entirely spoilt in consequence of the butter breaking through the edges while it is being rolled. As the difficulty experienced is generally to get the butter sufficiently cool, it is a good plan to place it upon ice before using it for the pastry. In hot weather the paste should be placed in a cool place a few minutes between each turn. If very flaky pastry is required, the paste may be brushed lightly over each time it is rolled with white of egg. Sift one pound of flour; put it on the pastry-board. Make a hole in the centre; add half a teaspoonsful salt and little less than half a pint of ice-water. The exact quantity of water cannot be given, owing to the difference in flour, but experience will soon enable you to determine when the paste is sufficiently stiff. Mix it in gradually with a knife, then work it lightly with the hands to form a smooth paste. Have ready three-quarters of a pound of butter. Flatten the paste till it is an inch thick; lay the butter in the centre, and fold over the four sides of the paste so as to form a square and completely hide the butter. Leave this to cool a few minutes, then dredge the board and the paste with flour, and roll the paste out very thin, and be especially careful that the butter does not break through the flour. Fold over a third of the length from one end, and lay the other third upon it. This folding into three is called giving one turn. Let the paste rest for a few minutes, then give it two more turns; rest again, and give it two more. This will be in all five turns, and these will generally be found sufficient. If, however, the pastry is to be used for patties, etc., six or seven turns will be required. Gather the paste together, and it is ready for use, and should be baked as soon as possible; and remember to dredge a little flour over it, the board, and rolling-pin every time it is rolled, to keep it from sticking. French cooks mix the yolks of two eggs with flour and water in the first instance. If a very rich paste is required a pound of butter to a pound of flour may be used.

CASSELL.

Paste.—One pound of flour, half a pound of butter, half a pound of lard. With a little water make a dough of the flour and lard; then roll it; spread a portion of the butter over it; fold and roll again; add more butter, and so on until you have used the half-pound all up.

You cannot make good paste out of poor flour. The "Perfection New Process Flour" will give you entire satisfaction.

Apple-pie.—Make a good crust and cover your plates with it. Pare, core, and cut up the apples in small pieces; put them on to stew in just water enough to cover them; quarter a lemon and stew with the apples. When soft mash the apples, remove the seeds if any, sweeten to taste, and flavor with nutmeg or ground cinnamon.

Sliced Apple Pie.—Make a good, light crust; wet the edge of the pie plate and lay a thin strip all round. Pare, core, and slice the apples; lay them on the paste with a little sugar, the juice of half a lemon; flavor with nutmeg. Lay a top crust over the fruit, and bake nearly three-quarters of an hour.

Apple Meringue Pie.—Prepare the pie as in the foregoing receipt, omitting the upper crust, and while the pie is baking prepare a méringue by beating up the whites of three eggs with three ounces of powdered sugar to a stiff broth; spread two-thirds of the mixture over the fire, and put the other third into a paper funnel or cornucopia, and by squeezing it decorate the pie according to fancy; dust sugar over it. Return it to the oven to set the méringue.

Apple-Custard Pie.—Beat up six eggs with a cupful of sugar; add them to three cupfuls of stewed apples (cold), and add gradually a quart of milk to the mixture; season with nutmeg; cover the pie-plate with a good crust, with the edge neatly arranged; fill the pie with the custard, and bake.

Mince-meat for Pie.—Shred and chop very fine two pounds of beef-suet; by dredging the suet occasionally with flour it chops more easily and does not clog; boil slowly, but thoroughly, two pounds of lean round of beef and chop fine (mix all the ingredients as they are prepared); stone and cut fine two pounds of raisins; wash and pick two pounds of currants; cut fine half a pound of citron; chop two pounds of apples, weighing them after they have been peeled and cored; a tablespoonful of salt, a teaspoonful of ground cinnamon, a grated nutmeg, a saltspoonful of allspice, half as much cloves, half an ounce of essence of almonds, a pint of brandy, and a pint of cider. This may be kept in a cool place all winter. If too dry add more cider.

Manufacturers are competing with each other in the preparation of mince-meat to such an extent that it is no longer economy to prepare your mince-meat at home. Most of our first-class hotels use the "Thanksgiving Brand," a genuine New England preparation. It is put up in five or ten pound buckets, and I consider it a great saving to families, both in time and materials, to secure their meat all ready prepared, when they know they can get a reliable article.

When you are about to make mince-pies moisten the meat with cider, port, brandy, or water.

Pumpkin Pie.—Cut the pumpkin into strips, and stew them in water enough to cover them nicely; when done pour off the water and press the pumpkin through a sieve; add to the pulp two quarts of milk, and nine eggs to every quart of pulp; sweeten with sugar (beat the sugar and eggs together), and season liberally with ginger and nutmeg; prepare the pie-plates with a crust as for custard pies; fill the plate with the mixture, and bake in a hot oven. Serve the pies when cold. After drawing off the water from the pumpkin cover the pot with a towel and let it stand half an hour on the back part of the range to dry out the moisture.

Fruit Pies.—The under-paste for fruit pies may be made of flour and lard, but the top is generally made of good puff-paste; it may cover the pie entirely or only in strips, according to fancy. Should the fruit require longer cooking than the paste, prepare it by stewing or simmering before filling the pies with it.

Custard Pies.—Line a well-buttered pie-plate with a good paste; arrange a thick pie rim round the edge of the plate; beat up four eggs with one cupful of sugar, and gradually add a pint and a half of milk; fill the pies while in the oven; grate a little nutmeg over them and bake about twenty minutes.

Lemon Cream Pie.—Boil a pint and a half of milk, and add three tablespoonfuls corn-starch dissolved in a little cold milk. Return the milk to the fire; take the juice of two lemons, four eggs, one cupful sugar, and two tablespoonfuls of butter. Beat these ingredients together, and add to the milk; flavor with a teaspoonful of extract of lemon and grated nutmeg; **pour the** mixture into the pies (prepared as for custard pies) and bake. When done remove from the oven and set it aside. Whip up the whites of four eggs to a froth, and gradually add a cupful of powdered sugar; spread two-thirds of the mixture on the pie, and put the other one-third into a cornucopia, and by squeezing it decorate the pie according to fancy. Return it to the oven a few minutes to set the méringue.

Lemon Cream Pie, No. 2.—One tablespoonful of corn-starch dissolved in cold water, one cupful of boiling hot water, one tablespoonful of butter, one egg, juice and rind of one lemon. Sweeten to taste, and set aside to get cold. Fill crust with this cream, and bake in a hot oven. M. G. H.

Orange Pie.—Work a teacupful of powdered sugar and a tablespoonful of butter to a cream. Mix a tablespoonful of corn-starch with a little cold water, and add a teacupful of boiling water; let it cook long enough to thicken, stirring constantly; then pour the mixture on to the butter and sugar. Grate the peel from half an orange, and chop the other half fine—first removing all the inner white skin. Add this to the former ingredients, also a beaten egg and the juice of an orange. Peel another orange, and slice it in little thin bits, being careful to remove all the seeds and the tough white skin. Line a pie-plate with nice paste and bake it until just done; then fill with the custard and orange slices, and bake long enough to cook the egg. A méringue made with the whites of two eggs, a pinch of salt, and two tablespoonfuls of powdered sugar, beaten to a stiff froth, will be an improvement. Spread it over the pie; sift powdered sugar on the top, and set it again in the oven until slightly colored.

English Plum Pudding.—Take six ounces of finely grated bread, and mix with them a pound of flour, a pound of beef suet floured and chopped fine, a teaspoonful salt, half a pound of granulated sugar, three-fourths of a pound of raisins stoned and chopped, three-fourths of a pound of washed currants, two ounces each of candied lemon and orange peel, two ounces of citron shredded, a quarter of a pound apple chopped fine, half an ounce of mixed spice, consisting of ground cloves, cinnamon, and grated nutmeg, and half a teaspoonful of fresh grated lemon-peel. Mix these ingredients thoroughly, and work the mixture into a stiff batter by adding to it five eggs beaten up with half a pint of rich milk and a gill of brandy; turn the mixture into a floured towel; shape it nicely; tie it up not too tightly, but leave room enough for it to swell. Put it into a saucepan of boiling water, and keep it boiling for five hours uninterruptedly. Have a kettle of boiling water ready to add to your saucepan as fast as the water evaporates. When done sift powdered sugar over it; pour a little brandy or Jamaica rum round it; set a match to the liquor, and send it to the table with a hard or brandy sauce.

Plum-Pudding Sauce.—Four ounces sugar and two ounces butter, well creamed together; then beat an egg well into it, with two ounces of brandy.

New England Plum Pudding.—Two pounds bread, four quarts milk, three pounds raisins, two grated nutmegs, three teaspoonfuls each of cinnamon and allspice, eight eggs, one cup sugar, and one cup molasses. Bake three hours.

M. G. H.

Plain Plum Pudding.—Flour six ounces of suet, and chop it fine; add a quarter of a pound of currants, the same quantity of raisins, half a teaspoonful salt, and a teaspoonful Royal Baking Powder; sift a pound of flour into the mixture; mix the dry ingredients thoroughly, and stir into them nearly a pint of milk with three tablespoonfuls of molasses; add a little mixed spice; shape the pudding nicely; tie it up in a floured towel, allowing room for it to swell, and boil three hours.

Boiled Pudding.—Take a cupful of chopped suet, a cupful of grated bread, and a cupful of washed currants; mix with two tablespoonfuls sugar, a teaspoonful of grated lemon-peel, a salt-spoonful salt, and grated nutmeg; beat up two eggs with half a cupful of milk, and work the mixture to a light paste; wring some small cloths out of boiling water, flour them, and tie in each a small portion of the mixture; plunge them into boiling water, let them boil quickly half an hour, turn them out on a hot dish, dash sugar over them, and serve with a sauce made of sweetened melted butter, with a teaspoonful of grated lemon-peel, nutmeg to taste ; a few spoonfuls of brandy will improve it.

Batter Pudding.—Beat the yolks and whites of four eggs separately, and mix them with six or eight ounces of flour and a salt-spoonful of salt. Make the batter of the proper consistency by adding a little more than a pint of milk; mix carefully; butter a baking-tin, pour the mixture into it, and bake three-quarters of an hour. Serve with vanilla sauce.

Vanilla Sauce.—Put half a pint of milk in a small saucepan over the fire; when scalding hot add the yolks of three eggs, and stir until it is as thick as boiled custard; remove the saucepan from the fire, and when cool add a tablespoonful of Thurber's double extract of vanilla and the beaten whites of two eggs.

Chocolate Pudding.—One quart of milk boiled with one ounce of grated chocolate; sweeten to taste, and flavor with vanilla. Boil thoroughly, and stand aside to cool fifteen minutes ; then stir in the yolks of six eggs, well beaten ; bake in a pudding-dish until it stiffens like custard. Beat the whites of six eggs, with six tablespoonfuls of powdered sugar, to a stiff froth, and spread over top of pudding; put in oven and brown quickly. M. G. H.

Crullers.—Half a pint of buttermilk, one cupful of butter, two cupfuls sugar, and three eggs; beat up the eggs and add the sugar and milk. Dissolve half a teaspoonful of saleratus in a little hot water; add to the mixture, with a teaspoonful salt, half a nutmeg grated, and half a teaspoonful of fresh ground cinnamon. Work in as much sifted flour as will make a smooth dough ; mix thoroughly; dredge the board, rolling-pin, and dough with flour; roll it out and cut it in rings or fingers, and fry in hot fat.

I have recommended buttermilk in the above receipt, knowing its excellent qualities; but the majority of housekeepers consider it utterly useless. The following from the *British Mail* is appropriate here: "As the butter which is taken from the milk is only the carbonaceous or heat-producing element, there are still left in it all the nourishing properties which make it so valuable as food. As a drink for men at work in the hot sun buttermilk is far preferable to cider, metheglin, switchel, or any preparation of beer whatever, as it is not only cooling and refreshing, but also strength-giving. Of course there are plenty of people, who are constantly dosing themselves with blood-searchers, liver-purifiers, and stomach-invigorators, who would laugh at the mention of buttermilk as a medicine, and yet if they could be once persuaded to try drinking a glass of that fresh beverage every day they would soon find a corrective of their poor appetites and 'clogged-up' livers. In a little book of 'Plain Directions for the Care of the Sick,' written by an intelligent physician of Philadelphia, who has under his medical supervision several charitable institutions, we find buttermilk mentioned as being very useful, especially in fevers, as an article of diet for the sick."

Baking Powder.—I have endeavored to recommend to my many readers a few articles used in cooking that my long experience as a caterer has taught me are the best. A good baking powder is a very important article to have in every household, but it is difficult to get a powder without the presence of alum.

The Brooklyn Board of Health, on motion of President Crane, the Sanitary Superintendent, was directed to procure samples of the various kinds of baking powders sold in Brooklyn, have them analyzed, and make a report thereon to the Board. Without going in detail into the constitution of baking powders, it will only be necessary to say that they are made with bicarbonate of soda, or carbonate of ammonia, and cream of tartar, chemically known as the bitartrate of potassa. But the lack of skill, resulting in lumps of soda in the product, led manufacturers to ascertain the proper proportion of these salts and to mix them, selling the compound as a baking powder. Some of the manufacturers, on account of the cheapness of alum, have introduced it as an ingredient into baking powder, and the report of the Brooklyn Board concludes as follows: " From a careful examination we are satisfied that the weight of evidence is against the use of alum in baking powders, and that the risks incurred in its use are too great to be incurred for the sake of cheapness alone. The mucous membrane of the stomach and the intestinal canal is a delicate structure, and materials which would produce no effect on the outside skin might irritate and inflame these organs."

Dr. Mott, the Government Chemist, in his review of the subject, makes special mention of having analyzed the Royal Baking Powder and found it composed of pure and wholesome materials. He also advises the public to avoid purchasing baking powders as sold loose or in bulk, as he has found by analyses of many samples that the worst adulterations are practised in this form. And I may cheerfully add that our first-class hotels use only the best of everything, not only in baking powders but in every article that enters their storerooms, and that Royal Baking Powder is the only baking powder they allow used in their bakeries, it being free from alum and other unwholesome ingredients.

Roly-Poly Pudding.—One quart of flour, one-half pound of suet chopped fine ; rub in a little salt with flour, wet with water, and then roll it out and spread any kind of fruit over it. Roll up, put in cloth, and boil one hour. M. G. H.

Roly-Poly Lemon Pudding.—Take the pulp from three lemons ; remove the pith and add to it an equal weight of sugar ; boil twenty minutes ; then set the mixture to cool. Chop up seven ounces of suet, and mix it with one pound of flour, a salt-spoonful of salt, and water enough to make a paste ; roll it out nearly an inch in thickness ; spread the lemon mixture upon it, and roll it into a long pudding; pinch the ends together, tie it in a floured cloth, put it into boiling water, and boil constantly for two hours. Serve with wine-sauce.

Marlborough Pudding.—Grate apples enough to make eight ounces; add to this eight ounces of fine white sugar which has been well rubbed on the rind of a large lemon, six well-beaten eggs, three tablespoonfuls of cream, the strained juice of three lemons, eight ounces of butter; add quantity at pleasure of orange-flower water, and the grated peel of an orange and a lemon; line the pie-dish with rich puff-paste, put in the mixture, and let it bake in a quick oven.

Macaroni Pudding.—Butter a pie-dish, and cover the bottom with two and one-half ounces uncooked macaroni; pour over it one quart of cold milk, add two tablespoonfuls of sugar, stir in two well-beaten eggs, and flavor with one teaspoonful of vanilla (double extract) or any flavoring desired. Put bits of butter over top, dust a little grated nutmeg over top, and bake slowly two hours and a half.

Steamed Arrowroot Pudding.—Mix two tablespoonfuls of Beatty's Bermuda arrowroot with one cupful of milk; flavor one pint and a half of milk with any desired flavoring, put it on the fire, and when it boils pour it upon the arrowroot; stir well, and when it is cool add three well-beaten eggs, one tablespoonful each of sugar and brandy; put it into a well-buttered mould, cover, and steam it one hour and a half; then turn it out on a dish, and arrange some preserves or jam neatly around it, and serve.

Almond Pudding.—Blanch and pound, with a little water, three ounces of sweet and four ounces of bitter almonds; add one pint of milk, three tablespoonfuls of sugar, a little grated nutmeg, one tablespoonful of flour mixed smoothly in a little cold milk, one tablespoonful of grated bread, two eggs well beaten, and the whites of two eggs whisked to a froth; pour the mixture into a buttered mould, cover, and boil quickly three-quarters of an hour; let it stand a few minutes before turning out of mould. Serve with vanilla sauce.

Bachelor's Pudding.—Beat up three eggs, flavor with essence of lemon and grated nutmeg, and add them to four ounces each of finely-minced apples, currants, grated breadcrumbs, and two ounces of sugar; mix thoroughly and boil in a buttered mould nearly three hours. Serve with following sauce.

Wine Sauce.—Boil the thin rind of half a lemon in one wineglassful of water till the flavor is extracted; then take it out and thicken the sauce by stirring into it one saltspoonful of rice, flour, or arrowroot which has been mixed in water or milk, a walnut of butter; boil a moment, then add half a tumblerful of good wine; let the sauce get quite hot without boiling, sweeten a little, and serve with the pudding.

Bird's-Nest Pudding.—Make the foundation of nest of blancmange or corn-starch; grate the rinds of three lemons, and arrange around the blanc-mange to represent straw; extract the contents of four eggs through a small hole and fill the egg-shells with hot blanc-mange or corn-starch; when cold break off the shells and lay the moulded eggs in nest. Serve with jam or preserves.

Harlan's Pudding.—Take three ounces each of butter, sugar, and flour; whisk two eggs thoroughly, and gradually mix with them the loaf-sugar, which must be rubbed well on the rind of a lemon before it is pounded; then add the flour and the butter partially melted, a salt-spoonful of salt, and a little grated nutmeg. Butter insides of several cups; put a little jam at the bottom of each, and fill them nearly full with the mixture; bake half an hour; turn them out and serve with wine sauce.

Cocoanut Pudding.—Beat two eggs with one cupful of new milk; add one-quarter of a pound of grated cocoanut; mix with it three tablespoonfuls each of grated bread and powdered sugar, two ounces of melted butter, five ounces of raisins, and one teaspoonful of grated lemon-peel; beat the whole well together ; pour the mixture into a buttered dish, and bake in a slow oven ; then turn it out, dust sugar over it, and serve. This pudding may be either boiled or baked.

Citron Pudding.—Sift two tablespoonfuls of flour and mix with the beaten yolks of six eggs ; add gradually one pint of sweet cream, a quarter of a pound of citron cut in small strips, and two tablespoonfuls of sugar; mix thoroughly, pour the batter into buttered tins, and bake twenty-five minutes. Serve with wine or vanilla sauce.

Eve's Pudding.—Beat six ounces of butter to a cream ; add six ounces of sifted flour and six of sugar ; separate the yolks from the whites of four eggs ; beat them till they are light, then add the beaten yolks and afterwards the whites to the batter; mix, and add half a dozen pounded almonds and the grated rind of one lemon. Fill small tins about half full; set them before the fire for a few minutes, and when they have risen place them in the oven and bake for half an hour. Serve with a sweet fruit sauce.

Sliced-Apple Pudding.—Mix two tablespoonfuls of arrowroot with one pint of cream ; add two tablespoonfuls of sugar; put in stew-pan and place over fire until it boils. Slice thinly apples enough to fill a large-sized dish, laying them in a dish with alternate layers of apples and sugar and small walnuts of butter; pour on a tumblerful of jam as next layer, and over all pour mixture of arrowroot. Bake in moderate oven twenty-five minutes.

Astor-House Pudding.—Mix one tablespoonful of flour with two of milk; pour over it one cupful of boiling milk flavored with one teaspoonful extract of vanilla; add one tablespoonful of sugar, a walnut of butter, and the yolk of an egg, beaten. Line the edge of pudding-dish with a rich puff-paste, and fill the dish two-thirds full with slices of sponge-cake over which a good jam has been spread ; pour the custard over them and bake in a moderate oven; when done take out. Beat up the whites of two eggs with nearly one cupful of powdered sugar; spread the méringue over the pudding, and sprinkle a little sugar over it; return it to the oven a few minutes until the méringue is fawn-colored, and serve in dish with clean, white napkin neatly bound around the sides.

A good wine-sauce may be served with it if desired.

Manhattan Pudding.—Dissolve a walnut of saleratus in one tablespoonful of hot water; mix one cupful of milk, three well-beaten eggs, two tablespoonfuls of flour (mixed with cold milk), one pinch of salt, and four ounces of chopped citron; add saleratus, and mix all thoroughly; pour the mixture into a buttered mould, tie mould in a floured cloth, boil one hour and a half, turn out, and serve with a fruit-sauce.

Manioca Pudding.—Three tablespoonfuls of manioca, one quart of milk, a little salt, one tablespoonful of butter, and two well-beaten eggs; sugar, spice, or flavoring to the taste. Mix manioca in half the milk cold, and, with the butter, stir on the fire until it thickens or boils; pour it quickly into a dish, stir in the sugar and the remaining milk, and when quite cool add the eggs, spice, and wine or other flavoring. This pudding may be varied by omitting the eggs and substituting currants, chopped raisins or candied lemon, orange or citron sliced. Bake half an hour in a moderate oven.

CAKES.

English Christmas Cake.—Sift five pounds of flour; mix with it one tablespoonful of salt, one pound and a half of butter, and half a pint of fresh brewer's yeast or five teaspoonfuls of baking powder; if yeast is used allow dough to rise before adding other ingredients; mix in three pounds of washed currants, one pound and a half of "A" sugar, a whole nutmeg grated, one quarter of a pound of chopped candied lemon-peel, one wineglassful of brandy, and four well-beaten eggs; butter the tins and line them with buttered paper; bake in a moderate oven for two hours. The quantity of brandy recommended will serve to keep these cakes fresh for an indefinite time.

Apple Snow.—Reduce half a dozen apples to a pulp; press them through a sieve; add half a cupful powdered sugar and a teaspoonful of extract of lemon; take the whites of six eggs, whip them for several minutes, and sprinkle two tablespoonfuls of powdered sugar over them; beat the apple pulp to a froth, and add the beaten egg; whip the mixture until it looks like stiff snow; then pile it high in rough portions on a glass dish, garnish with small spoonfuls of currant-jelly, and stick a sprig of green on top.

Almond Cake.—Blanch and pound in a mortar thoroughly eight ounces of sweet and one of bitter almonds; add a few drops of rosewater or white of egg every few minutes to prevent oiling; add six tablespoonfuls of sifted sugar and eight beaten eggs; sift in six tablespoonfuls of flour and work it thoroughly with the mixture, gradually add a quarter of a pound of creamed butter; beat the mixture constantly while preparing the cake, or it will be heavy; pour the mixture into a buttered tin (place a buttered paper between the tin and the cake), allowing room for it to rise, and bake in a quick oven. Should the oven prove too hot for it, and the cake be in danger of burning, cover it with paper for a few minutes.

Almond Sponge Cake.—Take half a pound of loaf-sugar, rub the rind of lemon on a few of the lumps, and crush the whole to a powder; separate the whites from the yolks of five eggs, beat the yolks, and add the sugar gradually; then beat the whites to a stiff froth; add it to the dish, and sift in flour enough to make a batter; add a tablespoonful of essence of almonds; butter and paper a tin, pour in the mixture until the tin is two-thirds full, and bake one hour in a moderate oven. The bottom of the tin may be studded with small pieces of almonds.

Zephyr Cakes.—Excellent tea-cakes. Wash the salt out of nearly a quarter of a pound of butter; add to it a quarter of a pound of powdered sugar and three well-beaten eggs, a teaspoonful of rosewater, and sifted flour enough to make a thin batter; stir it with a wooden spoon till the batter is perfectly smooth and so light that it will break when it falls against the sides of the mixing-bowl; fill well-buttered muffin-moulds (small) nearly half full with the mixture, and bake in a quick oven; serve hot with newly-made butter.

Columbia Cake.—Beat three-quarters of a pound of butter to a cream; add gradually a pound of sugar, four well-beaten eggs, a cupful of milk, half a grated nutmeg, a salt spoonful cinnamon, a wineglassful of brandy, nearly two pounds of flour, and half a pound of washed currants; beat these ingredients together twenty minutes. Dissolve a teaspoonful of saleratus in a few spoonfuls of hot water, and stir it into the mixture; butter the pan and line it with buttered paper, pour in the cake, and bake in a moderate oven.

Knickerbocker Cakes.—Beat half a pound of fresh butter to a cream; add half a pound of powdered sugar, three-quarters of a pound of sifted flour, a tablespoonful of orange-flower water and one of brandy, and four ounces of washed currants; add five well-beaten eggs, and beat the mixture until very light. Line some shallow cake-tins with buttered paper, pour in the mixture until they are half-full, and bake in a quick oven.

Cocoanut Cake.—One and a half cups of sugar, half a cup each of butter and milk, one cup of cocoanut grated fine, two cups flour, three teaspoonfuls of baking powder. Bake in pans with dry cocoanut sprinkled over the top (three cakes). M. G. H.

Olive Gingerbread.—Five and one-half cups of flour, two cups of molasses, one cup of sour cream, half a cup of butter, and two teaspoonfuls each of soda and ginger. M. G. H.

Chocolate Cake.—*Outside:* Half a cup of butter, two cups of sugar, one cup of cold water, three cups of flour, four eggs, whites and yolks beaten separately, and three teaspoonfuls of baking powder. *Inside:* Five tablepoonfuls of grated chocolate with enough cream or milk to wet it, one cupful of brown sugar, and one egg well beaten. Let it come to a boil, and then flavor with vanilla. Cake is made in layers like jelly cake. M. G. H.

Chocolate Macaroons.—Put three ounces of plain chocolate in a pan, and melt on a slow fire; then work it to a thick paste with one pound of powdered sugar and the whites of three eggs; roll the mixture down to the thickness of about one-quarter of an inch; cut it in small, round pieces with a paste-cutter, either plain or scalloped; butter a pan slightly, and dust it with flour and sugar in equal quantities; place in it the pieces of paste or mixture, and bake in a hot but not quick oven.

Whortleberry Cake.—One quart of flour, one cupful of sugar, one pint of berries, a little salt, and three teaspoonfuls of baking powder. Mix stiff with milk like biscuit.
M. G. H.

Whortleberry Cake, No. 2.—One cupful of sugar, two eggs, one and a half cupfuls of milk with half a teaspoonful of soda dissolved in it; butter size of an egg, one quart of berries, one teaspoonful of cream-tartar, and flour enough to make a stiff batter. Bake in muffin-rings or tins.

Cocoanut Pound Cake.—Beat half a pound of butter to a cream; add gradually a pound of sifted flour, one pound of powdered sugar, two teaspoonfuls of baking powder, a pinch of salt, a teaspoonful of grated lemon-peel, quarter of a pound of prepared cocoanut, four well-beaten eggs, and a cupful of milk; mix thoroughly; butter the tins, and line them with buttered paper; pour the mixture in to the depth of an inch and a half, and bake in a good oven. When baked take out, spread icing over them, and return the cake to the oven a moment to dry the icing.

Icing.—One cupful white sugar, enough water to dissolve it; set on the stove and let it boil until it will "hair"; beat the white of one egg to a stiff froth, pour the heated sugar on the egg, and stir briskly until cool enough to stay on the cake. The icing should not be applied until the cake is nearly or quite cold. This will frost the tops of two common-sized cakes.

Cream Cake.—Sift half a pound of flour into three ounces of creamed butter; add an even teaspoonful of baking powder, two tablespoonfuls powdered sugar, a pinch of salt, half a teaspoonful of grated lemon-peel, a cupful of cream that has turned a little, and beaten egg. Mix the batter, pour it into a buttered and papered tin, and bake in a moderate oven.

Windsor Cake.—Beat the yolks and whites of six eggs separately. Have ready the crumbs of three Vienna rolls soaked in milk, and squeeze dry; mix the crumbs with four ounces of melted butter, add the beaten yolks and two ounces crushed sugar, with a teaspoonful of grated lemon-peel; work the mixture, and add gradually two ounces each of raisins, almond paste, and candied orange-peel. Next add the frothed whites of eggs; butter and paper a shallow tin, and bake in a moderate oven. When done sprinkle powdered sugar over it. If preferred, chopped almonds may be sprinkled over the bottom of the cake-tin before adding the cake.

Ginger Cup Cake.—Mix two cupfuls of powdered sugar with two cupfuls of warmed butter; add three well-beaten eggs, a cupful of molasses, four heaping cupfuls of flour, a tablespoonful of fresh ground ginger, and a tablespoonful of dissolved saleratus; mix thoroughly, and pour into buttered moulds or patty pans. Bake in moderate oven.

Macaroons.—Blanch and pound six ounces of sweet almonds; add one pound of powdered sugar, the beaten whites of six eggs, two ounces of rice flour, and one tablespoonful of brandy; mix all well together, and drop the mixture in small quantities through a cornucopia on a sheet of confectionery paper, leaving a small distance between each, and bake in a moderate oven. It is best to bake one little cake at first, and if it is at all heavy add a little more beaten white of egg. A strip of blanched almond in the middle of each will be an improvement. They should be baked a fawn color.

Neapolitan Cake.—Blanch and pound to a smooth paste six ounces of sweet and one ounce of bitter almonds; add a few drops of orange-flower water while pounding to prevent oiling.; add a pinch of salt, the grated rind of one lemon, four ounces of butter from which the salt has been extracted, half a pound of crushed loaf-sugar, ten ounces of flour; mix thoroughly, and add the well-beaten yolks of six eggs after the eggs have cooled a little. Roll the paste out to the thickness of about one-quarter of an inch, and stamp out into small forms with a cake-cutter; lay them upon a floured tin, and bake in a good oven. When they are done take them out, and when cold cover the tops with a little icing. Return them to the oven one moment to dry the icing.

Marbled Cake.—One cupful of butter, two of sugar, three of flour, four well-beaten eggs, and one cupful of milk; two teaspoonfuls of baking powder; dissolve a large spoonful of chocolate with a little cream, and mix with a cupful of the batter; cover the bottom of your pan with the batter, and drop upon it in two or three places a spoonful of the chocolate, forming rings, then another layer of the batter, and so on until all is used. Bake in a moderate oven.

Pound Cake without Soda.—One pound powdered sugar, half pound butter, eight eggs, whites and yolks beaten separately and well; ten ounces flour, one nutmeg; bake one hour or longer. Never fails, and will keep one week.

Lady Fingers, No. 1.—Beat the whites and yolks of four eggs separately; mix with the yolks three ounces of flour and three of powdered sugar; add the beaten whites, and afterwards a gill of rose-water; beat all together a few minutes; put the mixture in a paper funnel, and squeeze it out into the shape of fingers on paper which has had a little powdered sugar dusted over it; dust a little sugar over the fingers; let them stand five minutes, then bake to a fawn-color in a moderate oven; fasten together after they have been baked with a little white of egg. Keep them in close-covered tin till wanted.

Lady Fingers, No. 2.—Rub half a pound of butter into a pound of flour; add half a pound of sugar; grate in the rinds of two lemons, and squeeze in the juice of one; then add three eggs; make into a roll the size of the middle finger; it will spread in the oven to a thin cake; dip in chocolate icing.

Crescents.—Mix three ounces of rice-flour with three ounces of powdered sugar; add three well-beaten eggs; mix all thoroughly, then spread the mixture thinly on paper and bake for twenty minutes. Take it out, and stamp into the shape of crescents; cover each crescent with icing, and return them to the oven for a minute or two to dry; add to a portion of the icing a little cochineal, to make some of the cakes pink-colored.

Maids of Honor.—One cup *each* of sour and sweet milk, one small cup of white pounded sugar-candy, one tablespoonful of melted butter, the yolks of four eggs, and the juice and rind of one lemon. Put both kinds of milk together in a vessel, which is set in another, and let it become sufficiently heated to set the curd; then strain off the milk, rub the curd through a strainer, add butter to the curd, also sugar-candy, well-beaten eggs, and lemon. Line the little pans with the richest of paste, and fill with the mixture; bake until firm in the centre—from ten to fifteen minutes.

Charlotte Russe.—Take one-fifth of a package of gelatine and half a cupful cold milk; place in a farina boiler, and stir gently over the fire until the gelatine is dissolved; pour into a dish, and place in a cool room; take one pint of rich cream and whisk it with a tin egg-beater until it is thick; flavor the cream with either vanilla or wine, and sweeten to taste; when the gelatine is cool strain carefully into the prepared cream; line a mould with ladyfingers; then pour the cream in carefully until it is filled; cover with ladyfingers.

Manioca Cream.—Three tablespoonfuls of manioca, one pint of milk, three eggs, vanilla and sugar to taste; soak the manioca in water till soft; boil the milk; while boiling stir in the manioca and the yolks of the eggs, beaten with the sugar; when cooked sufficiently, pour into a dish to cool; when cold, add the vanilla; beat the whites of the eggs till stiff, sweeten and flavor them, and stir part into the pudding, putting the rest on top.

Blanc-Mange.—Blanch ten bitter almonds with two ounces of sweet almonds, and pound them to a paste; add by degrees a third of a pint of cold water; let it stand till settled, and strain off the almond milk. Put into a pint of milk five ounces of loaf-sugar, three inches of stick vanilla, and pour it into an enamelled saucepan; boil slowly till the sugar is dissolved, then stir in an ounce of well-soaked isinglass; strain into a basin; add the milk of almonds with a gill of cream; remove the sticks of vanilla, and when cold pour the mixture into individual moulds and place in icebox till wanted.

Meringues.—Take one pound of powdered sugar, and add it to the beaten whites of eight eggs (slowly), until it forms a stiff froth; fill a tablespoon with the paste, and smooth it with another spoon to the desired shape; sift a little sugar over a sheet of paper, drop the meringues about two inches apart; dust a little sugar over them, and bake in a quick oven with door left open, so they can be watched constantly; when fawn-colored, take them out; remove them from the paper with a thin knife; scrape out of each a little of the soft part. They may be neatly arranged around a dish of whipped cream, or filled with ice-cream. If whipped cream is used, they would be improved by the addition of a little bright jelly inside each meringue.

Macaroon Basket.—This is a pretty and unconventional way of serving up macaroons with whipped cream, etc. Make a cement of sugar boiled to crackling, into which dip the edges of macaroons. Line a two-quart (deep) cake-pan with them, bottom and sides, taking care that the edges of macaroons touch each other firmly; also have a care not to pack them so tightly in the pan as to prevent easy removal. Set aside to dry, and when wanted fill with the desired cream, and serve on a glass dish.

Italian Cream.—Put one ounce of soaked isinglass, six ounces of loaf-sugar, half a stick of vanilla, and one pint of milk into a saucepan; boil slowly, and stir all the time until the isinglass is dissolved; strain the mixture, and when a little cool mix it with a pint of thick cream. Beat thoroughly until it thickens. Pour into a large or individual moulds, and put in ice-box until wanted.

Whipped Coffee Cream.—Sweeten one pint of rich cream rather liberally; roast two ounces of coffee beans; when they are lightly browned throw them into the cream at once and let the dish stand one hour before using; strain and whip the cream to a firm froth. A teaspoonful of powdered gum-arabic, dissolved in a little orange-flower water, may be added to give the cream more firmness, if desired.

Whipped Cream with Liqueurs.—Proceed as with coffee cream, flavoring the cream before whipping with Curaçoa, Maraschino, or any other cordial that may be desired. Other creams can be made on the same principle with chocolate extracts or highly-flavored wines.

Bavarian Cream.—Whip one pint of cream to a stiff froth and set in a colander one minute, to allow unwhipped portion to drip away; boil one pint of milk with a stick of vanilla and half a cupful of sugar until flavor is extracted; then take out stick of vanilla, and remove sauce-pan from fire;

add half a box of Cox's gelatine that has been soaked in water; add the well-beaten whites of four eggs, and when the mixture has become quite cold add the whipped cream gradually until it is well mixed; put into individual moulds a teaspoonful of some bright jelly or jam, then pour in the mixture and place in ice-box until wanted. This cream may be flavored in any way desired.

Ice-Cream.—Use only the best materials for making and flavoring. Avoid using milk thickened with arrow-root, corn-starch, or any farinaceous substance. Pure cream, ripe natural fruits, or the extracts of same, and sugar of the purest quality, combine to make a perfect ice-cream. In the first place secure a good ice-cream freezer. Of these several are made. Without recommending any particular make, we would suggest that one be secured working with a crank and revolving dashers. Next secure an ice-tub, not less than eight inches greater in diameter than the freezer. See that it has a hole in the side near the bottom, with a plug, which can be drawn at pleasure, to let off water accumulated from melting ice. Get a spatula of hard wood—not metal—with a blade about twelve inches long and four or five inches wide, and oval-shaped at end. This is used to scrape off cream which may adhere to the sides of freezer in process of freezing, also for working flavorings and fruits into cream. A smaller spade is also necessary for mixing salt and ice together and for depositing this mixture in the intervening space between can and ice-tub. Ice must be pounded fine in a coarse, strong bag. To freeze the cream, assuming it to be already flavored, first pound up ice and mix with it a quantity of coarse salt, in the proportion of one-third the quantity of salt to amount of ice used. Put freezing-can in centre of tub, taking care that lid is securely fastened down, and pile the mixed ice and salt around it on inside of tub to within three inches of top. First turn crank slowly, and as cream hardens increase the speed until mixture is thoroughly congealed, and revolving dashers are "frozen in." Remove the lid, take out dashers, cut away the cream which has adhered to the sides, and proceed to work the mixture with the spatula until it is smooth and soft to the tongue. Reinsert the dashers, cover can again, and work crank until entire contents are hard and well set. It is now ready to be served.

Vanilla Cream.—Four quarts of very rich cream, containing no milk; split two good-sized vanilla beans and cut up into small pieces; two pounds of powdered sugar and four fresh eggs; beat the eggs thoroughly in a porcelain-lined dish; add the sugar, and stir both well together; add the cream and throw in vanilla; place on fire, stirring constantly until boiling commences, but do not retain it there an instant after that time; strain through a hair sieve, and when cool pour it into the freezer and freeze.

Lemon Ice-Cream.—Grate off the yellow rind of two large fresh lemons, with half a pound of loaf sugar, using care not to grate a particle of the white, leathery pith beneath; crush the sugar to a powder, strain over it the juice of one lemon; add a pint of rich cream; stir until sugar is dissolved and freeze.

Peach Ice Cream.—Pound to a pulp twelve whole canned peaches; strain through a hair sieve and add six ounces of loaf-sugar which has been setting on fire to dissolve a few minutes; add one pint and a half of cream and a few drops of cochineal to give it a nice peach-color; freeze. Fruit creams of any kind can be made in same manner.

Water Ices.—*Lemon Ice:* Rub the rinds of six lemons upon twelve square lumps of sugar; squeeze over them the strained juice, half a pint of water, and a pint of syrup made by boiling three-quarters of a pound of sugar in nearly a pint of water; put in an earthen crock for one hour and a half, then mix, strain, and freeze. The ice will be improved by adding the whites of three eggs beaten to a froth with six ounces of powdered sugar. Serve in glasses.

Apricot Ice: Skin, divide, and stone six large ripe apricots; blanch, pound, and add the kernels to the fruit, with the juice of two lemons, half a pint of water and two ounces of clarified sugar; put in an earthen crock for one hour and a half, then strain and mix the whites of three eggs beaten to a firm froth with four ounces of powdered sugar; add this to the prepared water, mix thoroughly, and freeze.

Orange Basket.—Remove the fruit from interior of the orange carefully by making a small incision on one side of the orange, then cut the skin into shape of a basket, leaving about one half an inch of the stalk end for a handle. Fill the basket with ices, ice creams, frozen punches, whipped creams, jellies, etc. They look very pretty on a table. The fruit portion of orange can be utilized by removing the pith and seeds and sending to table sweetened with sugar, or used to make orange ice cream or ices.

Good Coffee.—The following remarks addressed to the trade by Messrs. H. K. & F. B. Thurber & Co. are so true and brief, yet so comprehensive, that I introduce them here:

"Nothing is more generally desired or appreciated, nothing harder to find, than a uniformly good cup of coffee. Its production is generally considered an easy matter, but it involves the observance of a considerable number of conditions by a considerable number of persons, and a volume might be written about these and still leave much to be said. We will, however, briefly state the most important requisites.

"The wholesale dealer must exercise care and judgment in his selections, as there is almost as much difference in the flavor of coffee as there is of tea; this is especially true of Mocha, Java, Maracaibo, and other fancy coffees, of which frequently the brightest and handsomest looking lots are greatly lacking in the flavor and aroma which constitute the chief value of coffee, and which can be ascertained only by testing carefully each invoice purchased. It should be roasted by a professional roaster, as this is a very important part of the programme, and requires skill, experience, and constant practice. Expert roasters are usually experienced men and command high salaries. A bad coffee-roaster is dear at any price, as the coffee may be ruined or its value greatly injured by an error in judgment or an instant's inattention. Owing to these circumstances, in addition to the fact that in order to do good work it is necessary to roast a considerable quantity at a time, none of the small hand-machines produce uniformly good results, and they are only to be tolerated where distance makes it impossible for the retail merchant to obtain regular and (when not in air-tight packages) frequent supplies of the roasted article. *How much* it should be roasted is also an important part of the question; for making "black" or "French" coffee, it should be roasted higher than usual (the French also often add a little chiccory), and some sections are accustomed to a higher roast than others, but as a whole the customary New York standard will best suit the average American palate.

"Retail dealers should buy their roasted coffee of a reliable house that has a reputation to sustain, and that cannot be induced to cut down prices below what they can afford to furnish an article that will do them credit; do not buy much at a time (unless in air-tight packages), a week or ten days' supply is enough, and if you are situated so you can buy it twice a week so much the better. Keep it in a dry place, and, if possible, in a tin can which shuts tightly, never in a pine box or bin, for the smell of the wood is quickly absorbed by the coffee. Get your customers in the habit of buying it in the berry, or, if they have no mill at home and want you to grind it for them (every grocer should have a mill), grind it pretty fine, so that when used the strength is readily extracted, but do not sell them much at a time, as it is a *necessity* to have coffee *freshly ground.*

"Consumers should adopt the above suggestions to retail dealers—buy of a reliable dealer who will not represent an inferior article as 'Java'; buy in small quantities, and buy often; keep it dry and in a tightly-closed tin can, or in a glass or earthen jar. Have a small 'hand coffee-mill,' and grind only when ready to use it; and if during rainy weather the kernels become damp and tough, warm them up in a *clean* pot or skillet, but do not scorch them; this drives off the moisture, restores the flavor, and makes it grind better.

The grinding is an important feature; if ground too coarse, you lose much of the strength and aroma of the coffee; if too fine, it is hard to make it clear, but of the two the latter is least objectionable; both the strength and flavor of the coffee, however, is a necessity, and if a little of the finely-powdered coffee flows out with the liquid extract, it is clean and will hurt nobody. It is better, however, to grind it *just right*, which is so that the largest pieces will be no larger than pin-heads.

"We now come to the important part of making coffee. For this there are many receipts and formulas, including a large number of new and so-called improved coffee pots, but we have never seen any of the new methods which in the long-run gave as satisfactory results as the following old-fashioned receipt:

"Grind moderately fine a large cup of coffee; break into it one egg with shell; mix well, adding just enough cold water to thoroughly wet the grounds; upon this pour one pint of boiling water; let it boil slowly for ten to fifteen minutes, and then stand three minutes to settle; pour through a fine wire sieve into coffee-pot, which should be first rinsed with hot water; this will make enough for four persons. *Coffee should be served as soon as made.* At table first rinse the cup with hot water, put in the sugar, then fill half full of *hot* milk, add your coffee, and you have a delicious beverage that will be a revelation to many poor mortals who have an indistinct remembrance of and an intense longing for *an ideal cup of coffee.* If you have cream, so much the better; and in that case boiling water can be added either in the pot or cup to make up for the space occupied by the milk, as above; or condensed milk will be found a good substitute for cream.

"*General remarks.*—We have thus briefly indicated the points necessary to be observed in obtaining uniformly good coffee, whether made from Rio, or Java, and other mild-flavored coffees. In the Eastern and Middle States Mocha, Java, Maracaibo, Ceylon, etc., are most highly esteemed and generally used; but at the West and in the South more Rio coffee is consumed. The coffee *par excellence,* however, is a mixture of Mocha and Java roasted together, and thus thoroughly blended. Mocha alone is too rough and acrid to suit many palates, but blended as above it is certainly delicious. In all varieties, however, there is a considerable range as to quality and flavor, and, as before stated, the best guide for the consumer is to buy of a reliable dealer, and throw upon his shoulders the responsibility of furnishing a satisfactory article.

"Hotels and restaurants that desire good coffee should make it in *small quantities* and *more frequently*. It is impossible for coffee to be good when it is kept simmering for hours after it is made."

"**A Cup of Coffee.**"—The author of "Salad for the Solitary," etc., has so well covered all the facts concerning the origin and history of this domestic beverage that little remains to be said; but as the establishment of the first coffee-house in London is connected with a curious anecdote, perhaps my readers will like to hear it.

Mr. D. Edwards, a Turkish merchant, on his return from Smyrna to London, brought with him a Greek of Ragusa, named Pasquet Rossee, who used to prepare coffee every morning for his master. Edwards's neighbors, beginning to appreciate the good qualities of this beverage, became so numerous as visitors at breakfast-time that in order to get rid of them he ordered Rossee to open a coffee-house, which the latter did in St. Michael's Alley, Cornhill. This was the first coffee-house in the city.

Now, taking its popularity as a basis, let us laugh at the doctors who maintain the theory that hot coffee irritates the stomach and injures the nerves. Let us tell them that Voltaire, Fontenelle, and Fourcroy, who were great coffee-drinkers, lived to a good old age. Let us laugh, too, at Madame Sévigné, who predicted that coffee and Racine would be forgotten together.—*Exchange.*

VEGETABLES.

Potatoes.—To boil a potato properly is very naturally supposed to be a very easy matter, but how seldom do we meet with one boiled to a proper turn ? In 1873, while out hunting in northwestern Minnesota, I stopped at an old log-cabin for dinner. The proprietor of the hostelry was an old down-East Yankee, who, suffering from a lung complaint, had taken his family out West, and had pre-empted one hundred and sixty acres, there to remain the rest of his days. I had the good fortune of having a well-filled pocket-pistol of brandy with me (to be used for medicinal purposes only), which I soon converted into milk-punch while his wife was preparing dinner. He was delighted with it, and told me that it was the first drop of spirits he had seen or tasted for several years (and I believed him, from the manner in which that punch disappeared). This set him to telling me what a splendid cook his wife was, and that she could beat "all tarnation a' biling taters." I left him immediately and offered my services to madam as second cook, my object being to learn her *trick* of boiling potatoes. At last dinner was ready, the cloth spread, and while the judge (as he was called) set the table I looked for a garden (?) to get a salad. Not finding the cultivated article, I had to resort to the field, and obtained a few edible weeds, washed and dried them, and prepared them for dinner.

OUR BILL OF FARE.

Vegetable Soup.
Smoked Shad with drawn Butter.
Roast Rump of Salted Beef.
Boiled Potatoes.
Parsnip Fritters.
Weed Salad.
Home-made Cheese. Cold Johnny-cake.
Acorn Coffee.

My long tramp over the prairie hunting prairie-chickens may possibly have had something to do with my ferocious appetite, but I do not remember an occasion when I enjoyed myself so much at table or ate so heartily. The dinner was a success, and the potatoes surpassed all expectations. I am not much of a potato-eater, but on this occasion I surprised myself by asking for a potato the third time.

Her receipt for boiling potatoes was very simple. She washed them well and peeled off a strip about a quarter of an inch wide lengthwise round each potato, placed them in an old iron pot, covered them with fresh rain-water (cold), and added a teaspoonful of salt. She allowed them to boil fifteen minutes, and then poured out a quart of the hot water and added a quart dipperful of cold water. When the edge of the peel began to curl up, she pronounced them done, and removed them from the pot, covered the bottom of a baking-tin with them, placed them in the oven with a towel over them for fifteen minutes, with the oven-door open. They were splendid.

The roast rump of salt beef was a new dish to me, but it was very good. It had stood in water twenty-four hours to extract the salt from it. It was a little dry and a trifle too well done.

My salad was composed of a few dandelions that had grown in a shady spot, a few inch dock-leaves, the tip-ends of the milk-weed, and a few wild chives, with bacon dressing; but I had no vinegar. As a substitute I gathered a handful of sheep sorrel, chopped it up fine, and sprinkled it over the salad.

On my departure the *judge* addressed me as Mr. Weed-eater, and requested me to make his cabin my home whenever I was in Minnesota.

Cabbage.—Never buy overgrown cabbages. They may appear very pleasing to the eye, but they are apt to be too coarse and too full of fibres to make a palatable dish. Do not trim off the outer leaves until the day they are wanted. It is a good plan to purchase a few dozen heads of cabbage with the stalks on, and hang them up in the cellar, heads down; then cut them down when wanted. Cut the heads into quarters; trim off all wilted leaves; cover them with cold water; add a handful of salt, and let them stand an hour before boiling. This process thoroughly cleanses them from insects, etc., that may be concealed between the leaves. When ready to boil cover them with boiling water; add a pea of soda, a little salt, and boil till tender. The old-fashioned way of boiling cabbage and other vegetables for a boiled dinner with the joint is not to be recommended for families outside of the farm, as it makes althogether too hearty a meal for those taking but little exercise.

Boiled Asparagus.—If the cut end of asparagus is brown and dry and the heads bent on one side, the asparagus is stale. It may be kept a day or two with the stalks in cold water, but it is much better fresh. Scrape off the white skin from the lower end, and cut the stalks of equal length; let them lie in cold water until it is time to cook them; tie the asparagus in small bundles, put them into a pot with plenty of water, and a handful of salt. When the asparagus is sufficiently cooked serve it on toast with drawn butter or with cream dressing, sauce vinaigrette, etc.

Boiled Artichokes.—Soak the artichokes and wash them in several waters; cut the stalks even; trim away the lower leaves, and the ends of the others; boil in salted water with the tops downwards, and let them remain until the leaves can be easily drawn out. Before serving remove the choke and send to table with melted butter.

Jerusalem Artichokes.—Peel the artichokes and throw each root into cold water and vinegar immediately, to preserve the color. Put them into boiling water, with a little salt, until sufficiently tender for a fork to pass through them easily; then pile them on a dish, and serve as hot as possible with melted butter or white sauce poured over. Soyer shaped them like a pear, then stewed them gently in three pints of water with two or three onions thinly sliced, one ounce of salt, and one ounce of butter. He then placed a border of mashed potatoes round a dish, stuck the artichokes in it points upwards, poured over them either white sauce or melted butter, and put a fine Brussels sprout between each. It made a pretty, inviting dish. Time to boil, about twenty minutes. They should be tried with a fork frequently after a quarter of an hour, as they will become black and tasteless if allowed to remain on the fire longer than necessary.

Brussels Sprouts.—Pick, trim, and wash a number of sprouts; put them into plenty of fast-boiling water. The sudden immersion of the vegetables will check the boiling for some little time, but they must be brought to a boil as quickly as possible, that they may not lose their green color. Add a tablespoonful of salt and a pea of soda, and boil very fast for fifteen minutes. Lose no time in draining them when sufficiently done; and serve plain, or with a little white sauce over the top.

Green Peas.—To have green peas in perfection, care should be taken to obtain them young, freshly-gathered, and freshly-shelled. The condition of the peas may be known from the appearance of the shells. When the peas are young the shells are green, when newly-gathered they are crisp, when old they look yellow, and when plump the peas are fine and large. If peas are shelled some hours before they are cooked they lose greatly in flavor.

Bottled Green Peas.—Shell the peas; put them into dry, wide-mouthed bottles, and shake them together so that they may lie in as little space as possible; cork the bottles closely, and seal the corks; bury the bottles in dry earth in the cellar, and take them up as they are wanted. They will keep three or four months.

Boiled Turnips.—Turnips should only be served whole when they are very young, and then they should be covered with white sauce. When they have reached any size they should be mashed. Pare the turnips, and wash them; if very young a little of the green top may be left on; if very large they should be divided into halves or even quarters; throw them into slightly-salted water, and let them boil gently till tender; drain and serve them.

Carrots.—This vegetable is almost invariably sent to table with boiled beef. When the carrots are young they should be washed and brushed, not scraped, before cooking—and old carrots also are better prepared in this way—then rubbed with a clean coarse cloth after boiling. Young carrots require an hour for cooking, and fully-grown ones from one hour and a half to two hours. The red is the best part. In order to ascertain if the root is sufficiently cooked, stick a fork into it. When they feel soft they are ready for serving.

Boiled Celery.—Have ready a saucepan of boiling water, with a little salt in it. Wash the celery carefully; cut off the outer leaves, make the stalks even, and lay them in small bunches; throw these into the water, and let them boil gently until tender, leaving the saucepan uncovered. When done, drain, and place them on a piece of toast which has been dipped in the liquid; pour over them a little good melted butter, and serve.

Boiled Spinach.—Take two pailfuls of spinach, young and freshly-gathered. Pick away the stalks, wash the leaves in several waters, lift them out with the hands that the sand or grit may remain at the bottom, and drain them on a sieve. Put them into a saucepan with as much boiling water slightly salted as will keep them from burning, and let them boil until tender. Take the spinach up, drain it, and press it well; chop it small, and put it into a clean saucepan with a little pepper and salt and a slice of fresh butter; stir it well for five minutes. Serve with the yolk of hard-boiled egg.

Onion.—This vegetable may be regarded either as a condiment or as an article of real nourishment. By boiling it is deprived of much of its pungent volatile oil, and becomes agreeable, mild, and nutritious. There is no vegetable about which there is so much diversity of opinion as there is about the onion, some persons liking a little of it in every dish, and others objecting to it entirely. Generally speaking, however, a slight flavoring of onion is an improvement to the majority of made dishes, but it should not be too strong.

Valuable Cooking Receipts. 95

The smell which arises from the esculent during cooking and the unpleasant odor it imparts to the breath of those who partake of it are the principal objections which are urged against it. The latter may be partially remedied by eating a little raw parsley before and after it. When onions are used for stuffing, the unpleasant properties belonging to them would be considerably lessened if a lemon, freed from the outer rind but covered as thickly as possible with the white skin, were put in the midst of them, and thrown away when the dish is ready for the table. Onions may be rendered much milder if two or three waters are used in boiling them. Spanish onions are not so strong as the English, and are generally considered superior in flavor. The largest are the best.

Boiled Beets.—Wash, but do not cut them, as it would destroy their sweetness; put them on to boil in a sufficiency of water, and let them boil from two to three hours, or until they are perfectly tender; then take them up, peel and slice them, and pour vinegar or melted butter over them. The root is excellent as a salad, and as a garnish for other salads it is desirable on account of the brightness of its color.

Boiled Corn.—Strip the ears, pick off the silk, and put them in a pot of water with a little salt; boil half an hour. When done, cut off the corn from the cob and season it with butter, pepper, and more salt if necessary, or serve on the ear.

Oyster-Plant.—Scrape the roots lightly; either cut them into three-inch lengths, or leave them whole, and throw them into water with a little lemon till wanted; put them into boiling salt and water, and keep them boiling quickly till tender; drain them, arrange on toast upon a hot dish, and pour over them good melted butter, white sauce, or sauce maître d'hôtel.

Boiled Cauliflower.—Cut the stalk close to the bottom, and pare away the tops of the leaves, leaving a circle of shortened leafstalks all round. Put the cauliflower head downwards into a little vinegar and water for a quarter of an hour. Put it into a pan of boiling water, with a tablespoonful of salt in it. Some persons prefer milk and water. Remove the scum carefully as it rises or the cauliflower will be discolored. Boil till tender. This may be ascertained by taking a little piece of the stalk between the finger and thumb, and if it yields easily to pressure it is ready. Drain, and serve. Put a lump of butter the size of an egg into a saucepan with a cupful of cold water; add gradually a teaspoonful of flour, mix smoothly, boil, and strain over the vegetable.

Boiled Horse Radish.—Cut each root into pieces two inches in length, and each piece into quarters; boil in water containing a little salt and one tablespoonful of vinegar. When tender drain, place the strips on a napkin, and send to table with drawn butter. This vegetable is seldom used except as a condiment or sauce ingredient. Although ignored in any other form, it is one of the most nutritious and healthful of all vegetables. It makes an excellent dish when used in equal portions with any vegetables handled in making fritters.

Stewed Cucumber.—Peel and quarter two cucumbers lengthwise; put them in a saucepan, add one teaspoonful of salt and one dozen whole peppers. When tender take them out; place them on toast, the edges of which have been dipped in water used in stewing. Pour drawn butter over them, well seasoned with cayenne pepper, and serve.

Stewed Dandelion.—The first mention of this dish will perhaps inspire most American people with aversion, but I can honestly advise them to try it. It is an inexpensive dish, and easily obtained; for fresh growths after showery weather may be had throughout the year. Gather a quantity of fresh dandelion; pick off all the withered tips and hard parts; shred them into strips, and wash them free from grit; put the dandelion into a stewpan with a strip of bacon, and add one tablespoonful of vinegar; cover it with a small quantity of boiling water, and stew until tender. Mash with a wooden spoon; stir in a lump of butter; flavor with pepper and salt, and serve like spinach. The dish may be garnished in a variety of ways, either with hard-boiled eggs, sippets of fried bread, or slices of boiled carrot cut into shapes. It is usually served with white meats, as veal, sweet-breads, etc., but it is excellent as a garnish for poached eggs.

The following weeds are all good greens if properly treated: the milk-weed, the different docks, fat hen, ox-tongue, jack-by-the-hedge, sea-holly (a substitute for asparagus), sea beet, shepherd's purse, sow thistle, hawk-weed, stinging nettle, willow herb, pile-wort, Solomon's seal, lamb's quarter, and a number of other weeds common to this country, and known only to a few. Once known they would be much sought after.

TABLE ETIQUETTE.

The following article from *Harper's Bazaar* is so appropriate under this head that we take the liberty of inserting it entire:

"TABLE ETIQUETTE.—There are a few points of table etiquette not directly connected with the giving and receiving of dinners and teas, but which are of the first importance, as they concern individual behavior. We would be inclined to think every one acquainted with them, and allusion to them a matter of supererogation on our part, if it were not that we see them so frequently violated. Those of our readers who are, or who have always been, familiar with them will perhaps pardon our speaking of them for the sake of those who are not.

"We do not expect to see these gaucheries in the best society; but there are many people perfectly well fitted for the best society but for ignorance concerning these things, which, although trifles in themselves, are of such infinite importance on the whole. For instance, where all the requirements are not fully known, if a general cessation of conversation should suddenly supervene upon the serving of the soup, would there be silence in the place? Not at all; the gap would be filled with a continuous bubbling sound from the mouth of some one or other unlucky wight whose mother never taught him to take soup properly, and who is possibly disturbing and disgusting all those that do better, and who know how easily the trouble might be avoided. Soup is to be taken from the side of the spoon, not from the tip, and it is not to be sucked in, but the spoon being slightly tilted, it is rather poured into the mouth than otherwise, the slightest silent inhalation being sufficient for the rest.

"Another generally neglected obligation is that of spreading butter on one's bread as it lies in one's plate, or but slightly lifted at one end from the plate; it is very frequently buttered in the air, bitten in gouges, and still held in the face and eyes of the table with the marks of the teeth on it. This is certainly not altogether pleasant, and it is better to cut it a bit at a time, after buttering it, and put piece by piece in the mouth with one's finger and thumb.

"Let us mention a few things concerning the eating of which there is sometimes doubt. A cream-cake, and anything of similar nature, should be eaten with knife and fork—never bitten. Asparagus—which should always be served on bread or toast, so as to absorb superfluous moisture—may be taken from the finger and thumb; if it is fit to be set before you, the whole of it may be eaten. Peas and beans, as we all know, require the fork only. Potatoes, if mashed, should be eaten with the fork. Green corn should be eaten from the cob; but it must be held with a single hand, and not after the fashion of the alderman's wife at the lord mayor's dinner. French artichokes are to be eaten with the fingers, slightly pulled apart at the top and one of the leaves pulled out with finger and thumb; the fleshy end of this leaf is then dipped in the salad dressing served with it, and only that atom of a paler color at the bottom of the leaf is taken as it peels off between the lips, when the dry portion is to be laid back in the plate. It is always served as a separate course by itself; a pretty hand looks very pretty indeed when fingering a French artichoke. Celery, cresses, radishes, and all that sort of thing are, of course, to be eaten from the fingers;

the salt should be laid upon one's plate, not upon the cloth. Fish is to be eaten with the fork, without the assistance of the knife; a bit of bread in the left hand sometimes helps one to master a refractory morsel.

"It is best to be very moderate in the beginning of a dinner, as one does not know what is to follow, and all the rest may be spoiled for one by an opposite course. We remember the case of a lady in Mexico, who, dining with the governor of the province, was served for the first course with a hash. She was somewhat surprised; but it was a very good hash, and she really made her dinner upon it. But the next course was also hash—there were seventeen courses of hash before the main dinner, of every delicious delicacy under the sun, made its appearance! Of course, a tiny morsel of each hash, for the sake of the flavoring, was all she should have taken; as it was, she sat afterwards like Tantalus.

"Berries, of course, are to be eaten with a spoon. In England they are served with their hulls on, and three or four are considered an ample quantity. But, then, in England they are many times the size of ours; there they take the big berry by the stem, dip it into powdered sugar, and eat it as we do the turnip-radish. It is not proper to drink with a spoon in the cup, nor should one, by the way, ever quite drain cup or glass. Spoons are sometimes used with puddings, but forks are the better style. A spoon should never be turned over in the mouth. Ladies have frequently an affected way of holding the knife half-way down its length, as if it were too big for their little hands, but this is as awkward a way as it is weak; the knife should be grasped freely by the handle only, the forefinger being the only one to touch the blade, and that only along the back of the blade at its root, and no further down. In sending one's plate to be helped a second time, one should retain one's knife and fork, for the convenience of waiter and carver. At the conclusion of a course where they have been used, knife and fork should be laid side by side on the plate—never crossed; the old custom of crossing them was in obedience to an ancient religious formula. The servant should offer everything at the left of the guest, that the guest may be at liberty to use the right hand. If one has been given a napkin ring, it is necessary to fold one's napkin and use the ring; otherwise the napkin should be left unfolded. One's teeth are not to be picked at table; but if it is impossible to hinder it, it should be done behind the napkin. One may pick a bone at the table, but, as with corn, only one hand is allowed to touch it; yet one can usually get enough from it with knife and fork, which is certainly the more elegant way of doing; and to take her teeth to it gives a lady the look of caring a little too much for the pleasures of the table; one is, however, on no account to suck one's fingers after it.

"Wherever there is any doubt as to the best way to do a thing, it is wise to follow that which is the most rational, and that will almost invariably be found to be the proper etiquette. There is a reason for everything in polite usage; thus, the reason why one does not blow a thing to cool it is not only that it is an inelegant and vulgar action intrinsically, but because it may be offensive to others—cannot help being so, indeed; and it, moreover, implies haste, which, whether resulting from greediness or from a desire to get away, is equally rude and objectionable. Everything else may be as easily traced to its origin in the fit and becoming.

"If, to conclude, one seats one's self properly at table, and takes reason into account, one will do tolerably well. One must not pull one's chair too closely to the table, for the natural result of that is the inability to use one's knife and fork without inconveniencing one's neighbors; the elbows are to be held well in and close to one's side, which cannot be done if the chair is too near the board. One must not lie or lean along the table, nor rest one's arms upon it. Nor is one to touch any of the dishes; if a member of the family, one can exercise all the duties of hospitality through servants, and wherever there are servants, neither family nor guests are to pass or help from any dish."

I would here disclaim against the disgusting habit of mouth-rinsing so prevalent at many dinner-parties. The bad taste of such a procedure seems to me so evident that everybody of refinement would avoid it. Yet I have repeatedly seen it resorted to in fashionable society.

BANQUET SERVICE.

The correct or proper manner of taking care of a number of guests that have assembled before the hour of dinner or supper has always been a puzzling problem to the novice in this line of business; but a first-class caterer will always be willing to help the host out of the dilemma, provided the host does not pretend to know more about the business than the caterer. It is a very good plan to have a colored servant at the door, another to receive the coat, hat, and cane, and give a paper check therefor, and still another to usher the guests to the reception-room, where they will find the host holding court over a bowl of lemonade or a light punch. The guests are eventually summoned to the banquet-room, but just before they enter it is "in good form" to serve them with a glass of plain Vermouth, or a Vermouth cocktail, as an appetizer. White servants are particularly to be recommended for the dining-room.

They then sit down to a repast, served in the following order (assuming of course that the table is set for a banquet):

No less than three, or more than five, oysters on the plate of each guest (with celery on table if in season). The oyster plates and forks are removed. Next serve the soups, with a grated rusk, plain roll, or French bread. *Hors-d'œuvres*, or whets, are now in order. Next serve the boiled releve; then the heavy entrée; after which serve the light entrée. Your guests will now expect the punch Roumaine, after which serve a good Russian cigarette (if gentlemen only). Then the roast joint; after which serve the game. Then the light salad, with a plain French dressing. Next the sweet entremet. The table should now be cleared; cheese and hard cracker offered; then the ices, with cake, etc., confectionery, dessert, coffee, liquors and cigars. The appropriate vegetables to be passed round with each joint or dish where they *naturally* belong.

The proper wines for above banquet are: with oysters, white Burgundies, Sauternes, and, if no other wine is at hand, a bottle of still Moselle may be served; with the soup, Sherry and Madeira; with the releves of fish, Hock wines; with the boiled joints, light Bordeaux (claret) and Burgundy wines; with the entrées, champagnes (though champagne may be served from the beginning to the end of dinner if asked for), after the last entrée serve the punch Roumaine, cardinal, etc., with cigarette if desired. A Rhenish wine may be on table to prepare the palate for the roast, and to counteract the sweetness of the punch. With the roasts and game heavy Burgundy and Bordeaux. At many English banquets port wine is sprinkled over the lettuce, and cheese and crackers are served at the same time, but it is not a modern custom. With the sweets, sherry and Madeira. A spoonful of brandy added to the coffee will aid digestion.

A *pony* of half green Chartreuse and S. O. P. brandy is excellent at the end of a dinner.

Serve the punch Roumaine after the last entrée, and not after the *roast*, as I have occasionally seen it on bills of fare.

Remember that venison cools rapidly. Iced or cold wines should not be served with it. Hot plates should not be forgotten.

Rhine wine takes kindly to boiled or roast ham.

Have you tried blanched almonds sautéed with a little butter, and seasoned with salt and pepper, and served after the cheese?

But one might suggest in this way indefinitely. The subject is inexhaustible.

Remarks on Wines.—A guest should not be censured "by looks" from the host if he refuses to drink any other wine than that served with the first course, provided it is of a good vintage and pleases his palate. Good, honest wines should be served at all large entertainments, but "private stock" and "rare vintages" should be reserved for the more private affairs, where the guests are personal friends of the host, and, though not recognized as wine-drinkers, they are good judges of and appreciate thoroughly a good glass of wine. The promiscuous gathering (with few exceptions) seldom appreciates a rare bottle of still wine. Their ideal wine is the champagne. I have often seen a bottle of splendid Château Yquem and Johannesberger pushed aside as "stuff" the moment the champagne appeared, and by gentlemen whom I had previously considered *bon vivants*. They will tell you that a wine with a deposit or crust cannot be pure, and it is only a waste of time to attempt to explain that old wines without a deposit are more or less *doctored*.

The host should be censured for sending his cellar curiosities to table when the majority of the guests are strangers to him.

On decanting wines, Denman has observed: "To fully develop the flavor and bouquet of any wine a little gentle warmth is necessary, and it is therefore advisable that the wines intended for immediate use should be placed in a warmer temperature than that of the cellar"; and Fin-Bec adds "that the dining-room is the proper place," which is the custom among first-class caterers. The heavy wines should remain in the dining-room uncorked a few hours under the supervision of a trusty person, for the average waiter is partial to good wine, and can remove a bottle as dexterously as a king of legerdemain.

Francatelli insists that the different kinds of sherries, ports, Maderia, and all Spanish and Portuguese wines are improved by being decanted several hours before dinner.

His advice and suggestions are proper; but does it not please the eye—is there not an unwritten history in all the dark cobwebs, etc., that cling with a brotherly affection to the original bottle?

The favorite Hocks with Americans are P. A. Mumm's Johannesberg, Barton & Guestier's, Henkell & Co.'s wines, and a few other well-known reliable firms. Prince Metternich,

Schloss Johannesberg wines are very good, but "Blue Seal" is held at too high a figure ($150 per case) to ever become popular.

P. A. Mumm's Hock wines are favorites, and justly so, for they are entirely free from adulteration.

At an American banquet recently given in London, the favorite wine was Heidsieck, on the ground that it was one of the first wines to find popular favor in America. This information will, no doubt, surprise wine-drinking Americans, for if our custom-house reports of importation are reliable, we have discovered several Rheims wines that are decidedly superior to Heidsieck. The importation in 1879 of G. H. Mumm's champagne alone was twenty-two thousand five hundred and twenty-six cases MORE than of any other brand.

Pommery and Cliquot (the two widows), Roederer dry, Moët & Chandon, Imperial, and a few others are all good dinner wines.

Sparkling Hock, if properly handled, is a wine that should find favor in this country, but the demand is so limited that it is very apt to spoil before the case is used up. That made from the Riesling grape is the best.

American champagnes (and it grieves me to say it) are not the proper wines to serve at a banquet or dinner. Their peculiar acrid taste does not suit a palate that has been educated on foreign wines. They may be served at a banquet given in a foreign country where every dish and every wine is purely American, or sent to the cook for his champagne (?) sauce, etc. A bottle of "Cook's Imperial" may be served at lunch, and it is proper enough at the end of the bar where the crackers and cheese hold court. It finds favor with the youth "seeing the sights" of a great city, but not elsewhere.

Pierre Blot, in the *Galaxy*, observed "that American wines are just as good as foreign wines for the table and for cooking purposes. Bogus wines," he said, "are sold to native Americans almost entirely." Friend Blot evidently got in with the *wrong crowd* when he visited us.

The First Champagne.—It happened that about the year 1668 the office of cellarer was conferred upon a worthy monk named Perignon. Poets and roasters, we know, are born, and not made; and this precursor of the Moëts and Cliquots, the Heidsiecks and the Mumms of our days, seems to have been a heaven-born cellarman, with a strong head and a discriminating palate. The wine exacted from the neighboring cultivators was of all qualities, good, bad, and indifferent; and with the spirit of a true Benedictine, Dom Perignon hit upon the idea of "marrying" the produce of one vineyard with that of another. He had noted that one kind of soil imparted fragrance and another generosity, and discovered that a white wine could be made from the blackest grapes, which would keep good, instead of turning yellow and degenerating like the wine obtained from white ones. Moreover, the happy thought occurred to him that a piece of cork was a much more suitable stopper for a bottle than the flax dipped in oil which had heretofore served that purpose. The white, or, as it was sometimes styled, the gray wine of Champagne grew famous, and the manufacture spread throughout the province, but that of Hautvillers held the predominance. The cellarer, ever busy among his vats and presses, barrels and bottles, alighted upon a discovery destined to be far more important in its results. He found out the way of making an effervescent wine, a wine that burst out of the bottle and overflowed the glass, that was twice as dainty to the taste, and twice as exhilarating in its effects. It was at the close of the seventeenth century that this discovery was made, when the glory of the Roi Soleil was on the wane, and with it the splendor of the court of Versailles. The king for whose especial benefit liquors had been invented found a gleam of his youthful energy as he sipped the creamy, foaming vintage that enlivened his dreary tête-à-tête with the widow of Scarron. It found its chief patrons, however, among the bands of gay young roysterers, the future *roués* of the Regency, whom the Duc d'Orléans and the Duc de Vendôme had gathered round them at the Palais Royal and at Anet. It was at one of the famous *soupers* d'Anet that the Marquis de Sillery, who had turned his sword into a pruning-knife and applied himself to the cultivation of his paternal vineyards on the principles inculcated by the cellarer of St. Peter's, first introduced the wine bearing his name. The flower-wreathed bottles which, at a given signal, a dozen of blooming young damsels scantily draped in the guise of Bacchanals placed upon the table were hailed with rapture, and thenceforth sparkling wine was an indispensable adjunct at all the *petits soupers* of the period. In the highest circles the popping of champagne-corks seemed to ring the knell of sadness, and the victories of Marlborough were in a measure compensated for by this grand discovery.—*London Society.*

MIXED DRINKS.

My receipts under this head are inserted for the benefit of *the gentlemen*, many of whom in the course of my experience have bewailed their lack of knowledge on this point when wishing to entertain their male friends at home.

Lemonade.—Take half a pound of loaf-sugar and reduce it to a syrup with one pint of water; add the rind of five lemons and let stand an hour; remove the rinds and add the strained juice of the lemons; add one bottle of "Apollinaris" water, and a block of ice in centre of bowl. Peel one lemon and cut it up into thin slices, divide each slice in two, and put in lemonade. Claret or fine cordials may be added if desired. Serve with a piece of lemon in each glass.

Milk Punch.—For a small party: Dissolve half a pound of sugar in a little hot water which has been flavored slightly with a little lemon peel; add the syrup to two quarts of rich milk (cream is preferable); pour in one pint of brandy and one gill of Jamaica rum; mix thoroughly, dust a little grated nutmeg over it, and set it in a cool place. Beat the whites of four eggs to a stiff froth with a little sugar and float on top of punch same as with egg-nogg. Sprinkle a little confectionery sugar over froth. Place a small piece of ice in each tumbler when serving.

Egg-nogg.—For a small party: Separate the yolks and

whites of twelve eggs; beat the yolks thoroughly, add two heaping cupfuls of sugar and half a grated nutmeg; beat the whole together thoroughly; add half a pint of brandy, half that quantity of Jamaica or Santa Cruz rum, and two quarts of rich milk. Beat up the whites of six of the eggs to a stiff froth, float it on top of mixture, and dust with a little confectioner's sugar. Place a piece of ice in each tumbler when serving.

Hot Tom and Jerry.—Separate the yolks and whites of ten eggs. Beat the yolks up thoroughly and add gradually four pounds of sugar. Beat up whites of eggs to a stiff froth and add gradually to above mixture. Flavor this batter with one wineglassful of Maraschino and a little nutmeg. Put one tablespoonful of this mixture into a china mug with a wineglassful of brandy and one tablespoonful of rum, and fill up the mug with hot water, stir well and dust a little more grated nutmeg over it if desired. Sherry may be used instead of brandy if preferred.

Hot Apple Toddy.—Heat a tumbler with hot water; throw out the water; put in one teaspoonful of sugar and one wineglassful of apple brandy; fill glass two-thirds full with hot water, add one quarter of a warm baked apple, a trifle of grated nutmeg, and send to table with spoon in the glass and some hard water crackers.

Hot Spiced Rum.—Heat a glass with a little hot water; throw out the water; put in one teaspoonful of sugar, one wineglassful of rum, a walnut of butter, three whole allspice, one clove, and fill up with hot water. Dust a little grated nutmeg over top if desired. Substitute Scotch whiskey for rum if preferred.

Santa Cruz Punch.—Place the juice of two lemons, one heaping tablespoonful of sugar, and a little water in a tumbler; stir a few minutes to dissolve the sugar; add a wineglassful of Santa Cruz rum; fill up the goblet with fine ice; add a slice each of orange, lemon, and pineapple. Stir well and serve with straws.

The favorite brands of whiskies are the famous "Old Crow" Bourbon, "Hermitage" and "Monongahela Monogram" rye.

Orange Co., N. Y., apple-jack is superior to that made in New Jersey.

Have you tried the sherries from the oldest house in Spain —Juan Gmo. Burdon? They are excellent. Served with our favorite dish, terrapin, the epicure exclaims: "The eternal fitness of things!"

PRESERVING, ETC.

It is not many years since every good housewife felt called upon at least once a year to take a great deal of trouble in preserving a supply of fruit for use during the winter months. The purchase of fruit-jars, the picking, or purchase, and sorting of fruit, the purchase of sugar, the boiling and preparation of the syrup, oftentimes in the hottest weather, was a task which many a good housewife looked forward to with some trepidation, while the uncertainties attending the keeping qualities of the preserves, after they were manufactured, made this a rather undesirable feature in housekeeping.

Within a few years, however, all this has become unnecessary; the manufacture of preserves on a large scale, with skilled labor and improved appliances, has proven, as in many other branches of manufacture, a great success; and while there are some thrifty housewives who still think their "home-made" preserves are better than the "store" article, it is undoubtedly true that the high-class preserves, such as are sold by Thurber, Park & Tilford, Acker, Merrall & Condit, and other first-class grocers, are decidedly fine, and in a number of cases far more appetizing and delicate than the home-made article. I say this with all due respect for the skill shown by many careful, conscientious housewives throughout the land, but in this case the doctrine "survival of the fittest," I think, is quite applicable. Too many people are apt to sit down, fold their hands, and disclaim against anything not made at home, at least as far as preserves and candied fruits are concerned. The sword, I must admit, cuts both ways. While I have wrestled carefully and conscientiously at many houses with *alleged* preserves made at home, I have suffered the "pangs of Tantalus" from atrocious compounds put on the market by conscienceless manufacturers. For the benefit of those who desire to "do up" their own fruits I append a few trustworthy receipts. For preserving, the "Almy jar" is particularly to be recommended.

In using this jar, fill it with the desired fruit while cold. Make a syrup of sugar (quantity as given below) by boiling well to prevent fermentation, or it can be put on fruit dry. Fill jar with fruit, pour sugar over it until jar is full halfway up the neck; screw on covers of jars without rubber rings; put a board indented with holes in botton of washboiler and stand jars on it; fill boiler with cold water up to neck of jars; boil (time necessary for different fruits is given below), then remove jars one by one, take off covers, fill with boiling water, put on rubber-rings and screw covers on tightly as possible. The same process is used in preserving all kinds of fruits.

PREPARING FRUITS FOR PRESERVING.

Boil Cherries moderately	5	minutes.
" Raspberries "	6	"
" Blackberries "	6	"
" Plums "	10	"
" Strawberries "	8	"
" Whortleberries	5	"
" Pie-Plant sliced	10	"
" Small Sour Pears, whole	30	"
" Bartlett Pears, in halves	20	"
" Peaches "	8	"
" Peaches, whole	15	"
" Pineapple, sliced ½ inch thick	15	"
" Siberian or Crab Apple, whole	25	"
" Sour Apples, quartered	10	"
" Ripe Currants	6	"
" Wild Grapes	10	"
" Tomatoes	90	"

Pour into warm jars.

The amount of sugar to a quart jar should be:

For Cherries	6 ounces.
" Raspberries	4 "
" Lawton Blackberries	6 "
" Field "	6 "
" Strawberries	8 "
" Whortleberries	4 "
" Quince	10 "
" Small Sour Pears, whole	8 "
" Wild Grapes	8 "
" Peaches	4 "
" Bartlett Pears	6 "
" Pineapples	6 "
" Siberian or Crab Apples	8 "
" Plums	8 "
" Pie-Plant	10 "
" Sour Apples, quartered	6 "
" Ripe Currants	8 "

Cider may be kept fresh and sweet by simply heating it until it throws off steam, then putting into hot jars and sealing immediately.

Apple Sauce ready for table use or pies may be preserved by putting in hot jars and sealing at once. Remember cold fruit requires cold jars, hot fruit requires hot jars.

To open the Jar.—Take the blade of a penknife, or any other thin instrument, and push the rubber in towards the neck at the O on the shoulder of the jar. The air will enter and the lid will easily unscrew.

Currant Jelly.—One pound of granulated sugar to each pint of juice. Squeeze the currants and boil juice twenty minutes, then add sugar, which should be heating while the juice boils; stir well together until sugar is well dissolved.

M. G. H.

Wine Jelly.—One box of Cox's gelatine, dissolved in one pint of cold water, one pint of wine, one quart of boiling water, one quart of granulated sugar, and three lemons.

M. G. H.

In making Jam, the first thing to be looked after is the fruit. As a general rule, this should be fully ripe, fresh, sound, and scrupulously clean and dry. It should be gathered in the morning of a sunny day, as it will then possess its finest flavor. The best sugar is the cheapest; indeed, there is no economy in stinting the sugar, either as to quality or necessary quantity, for inferior sugar is wasted in scum, and the jam will not keep unless a sufficient proportion of sugar is boiled with the fruit. At the same time too large a proportion of sugar will destroy the natural flavor of the fruit, and in all probability make the jam candy. The sugar should be dried and broken up into small pieces before it is mixed with the fruit. If it is left in large lumps it will be a long time in dissolving, and if it is crushed to powder it will make the jam look thick instead of clear and bright. The quantity to be used must depend in every instance on the nature of the fruit. Fruit is generally boiled in a brass or copper pan uncovered, and this should be kept perfectly bright and clean. Great care should be taken not to place the pan flat upon the fire, as this will be likely to make the jam burn to the bottom of the pan. If it cannot be placed upon a stove-plate, set it upon a slab of soap-stone or marble over the fire. Glass jars are much the best for jam, as through them the condition of the fruit can be observed. Whatever jars are used, however, the jam should be examined every three weeks for the first two months, and if there are any signs of either mould or fermentation it should be boiled over again. If you do not want to use the patent glass jar, the best way to cover jam is to lay a piece of paper the size of the jar upon the jam, to stretch over the top a piece of writing-paper or tissue-paper which has been dipped in white of egg, and to press the sides closely down. When dry, this paper will be stiff and tight like a drum. The strict economist may use gum dissolved in water instead of white of egg. The object aimed at is to exclude the air entirely. Jam should be stored in a cool, dry place, but not in one into which fresh air never enters. Damp has a tendency to make the fruit go mouldy and heat to make it ferment. Some cooks cover the jam as soon as possible after it is poured out, but the generally-approved plan is to let the fruit grow cold before covering it. In making jam, continual watchfulness is required, as the result of five minutes' inattention may be loss and disappointment.

Canning Tomatoes.—Scald your tomatoes; remove the skins, cut in small pieces, put in a porcelain kettle, salt to taste, and boil fifteen minutes; have tin cans filled with hot water; pour the water out and fill with tomatoes; solder tops on immediately with shellac and rosin melted together. M. G. H.

In canning, it is customary at hotels to follow the same process as in preserving, with the exception that not nearly so much sugar is used.

To Can Quinces.—Cut the quinces into thin slices like apples for pies. To one quart jarful of quince take a coffee-saucer and a half of sugar and a coffee-cup of water; put the sugar and water on the fire, and when boiling put in the quinces; have ready the jars with their fastenings, stand the jars in a pan of boiling water on the stove, and when the quince is clear and tender put rapidly into the jars, fruit and syrup together. The jars must be filled so that the syrup overflows, and fastened up tight as quickly as possible.

Green Tomato Pickle.—One peck green tomatoes sliced, six large onions sliced, one tea-cup of salt over both; mix thoroughly and let remain over-night; pour off liquor in the morning and throw it away; mix two quarts of water and one of vinegar, and boil twenty minutes; drain and throw liquor away; take three quarts of vinegar, two pounds of sugar, two tablespoonfuls each of allspice, cloves, cinnamon, ginger, and mustard, and twelve green peppers chopped fine; boil from one to two hours. Put away in a stone crock. M. G. H.

Chili Sauce.—Eight quarts tomatoes, three cups of peppers, two cups of onions, three cups of sugar, one cup of salt, one and one-half quarts of vinegar, three teaspoonfuls of cloves, same quantity of cinnamon, two teaspoonfuls each of ginger and nutmeg; boil three hours; chop tomatoes, peppers, and onions very fine; bottle up and seal. M. G. H.

Hot Sauce.—Six tablespoonfuls of sugar, two tablespoonfuls of butter, one egg; beat butter, sugar, and yolks together, the white, beaten to a stiff froth; add a teacupful of boiling water and one teaspoonful of vanilla. M. G. H.

The best way to prepare a new iron kettle for use is to fill it with clean potato parings; boil them for an hour or more, then wash the kettle with hot water, wipe it dry, and rub it with a little lard; repeat the rubbing for half a dozen times after using. In this way you will prevent rust and all the annoyances liable to occur in the use of a new kettle.

A new antiseptic is described by the *Journal of Chemistry*. It is a double salt of borate of potassium and sodium; and is made by dissolving in water equal portions of chloride of potassium, nitrate of sodium, and boracic acid, filtering and evaporating to dryness. It does not give a bad taste to food. Butter may be kept sweet by it at ordinary temperatures for a week. Meat, game, etc., dipped in a weak solution remain pure for a long time. A piece of meat well rubbed with the salt and laid away two years ago is now in perfectly good condition. Eggs dipped in a solution of this antiseptic remain good for a long period.

Morning Tonic.—An agreeable and effective tonic for the correction of any discomfort arising from a too heavy supper the night before may be taken in the morning before breakfast, as follows: One wineglassful of "Hunyadi Water," fifteen minutes afterward a goblet of "Apollinaris Water"; wait half an hour before breakfasting. The use of any alcoholic beverages before breakfast, such as cocktails, etc., is to be deprecated, as, aside from any moral point, it tends to promote indigestion, creates a false appetite, and is in every way injurious to the system. The man who resorts to it for "toning up," or as an "appetizer," deceives himself.

Dyspepsia Cure.—One-half an ounce each of pepsin and bismuth, one-quarter of an ounce cubebs, and two and a half grains lime; mix well and take a pinch of the powder fifteen minutes after each meal. I have never known this remedy to fail when tried. T. J. M.

MENUS.

My object in introducing the following menus is to serve a double purpose: first, to show progress made in the art of constructing menus in the past thirty years—for it is an art, and a very important one, too—among leading caterers; and second, to furnish hints to all who may wish to give dinners or suppers more or less elaborate. It has often happened in my experience that customers would submit to me bills of fare constructed by another caterer in the event of a prospective "spread," and say there was something about it they did not like, some dish they would like to substitute, etc. In this small space I have only attempted to give a few of the many thousand varieties in my collection, but I now have in preparation a volume embodying bills of fare, estimates for cost of different bills based on number of guests to be seated, together with a glossary or dictionary of French idioms and words used in menus and the reason of their adoption. The use of any but our own language on bills of fare ought to be avoided, but there are cases where it is impossible, and it is with the view of enlightening those who cannot understand the meaning of French terms used, and yet shrink from displaying their lack of knowledge, that I have devoted my time to the construction of a glossary.

DINNER ON THE ANNIVERSARY OF THE BIRTH OF DANIEL WEBSTER.

AT THE REVERE HOUSE, BOSTON, FRIDAY, JAN. 18, 1856.

Oysters on Shell.

Soup.

Mock Turtle.   Tomato.   Fish Chowder.

Fish.

Boiled Cod's Head and Oysters.
Fried Sea Trout with Rashers of Pork.
Baked Striped Bass, Stuffed, Claret Sauce.

Valuable Cooking Receipts.

Removes.

Roast Turkey. Boiled Turkey and Oyster Sauce.
Roast Sirloin of Beef. Boiled Capons and Pork, Celery Sauce.
Roast Mongrel Geese from Marshfield.
Boiled Leg English Mutton, Caper Sauce.
Roast Westphalia Ham, Champagne Sauce.

Cold Ornamental Dishes.

Boar's Head on a Soclé, Decorated.
Lobster Salad, Garnished, in Jelly. Galatine of Turkey with Truffles.
Quail with Plumage, on Form. Boned Chicken with Truffles.
Pate of Liver in Jelly. Aspic of Oysters, a la Royale.

Entrees.

Macaroni a la Anizine. Mutton Cutlets, Breaded.
Venison Steak, Jelly Sauce. Vol au Vent, a la Financiere.
Arcade of Partridge with Olives.
Terrapin, Stewed, Port Wine Sauce.
Fillets of Black Grouse with Truffles.
Sweetbreads, Larded, with Green Peas.
Veal Cutlets, Larded, Tomato Sauce.
Mutton Kidneys, Champagne Sauce..
Fillet of Beef with Mushrooms. Turban of Fillets of Chicken.
Calf's Head, Turtle Sauce. Oysters Fried in Crumbs.
Tripe, Webster Style.

Game.

Gray Ducks. Canvas-Back Ducks. Black Ducks.
Widgeons. Partridge. Red Heads. Prairie Grouse.
Quail. English Pheasants. Teal. Brant.

Meringue Baskets. Omelet Soufflee. Blanc-Mange. Pastry.
Creams. Confectionery. Wine Jelly. Charlotte Russe.

ORNAMENTS.

Dessert.

Lemon Ice-Cream. Fruit. Frozen Plum-Pudding.
Roman Punch. Bon-Bon Glace.

Coffee and Liqueurs.

Valuable Cooking Receipts.

BANQUET AT THE TENTH ANNUAL REUNION OF THE SOCIETY OF THE ARMY OF THE CUMBERLAND.

FRIDAY, JULY 7, 1876, ST. GEORGE'S HALL, PHILADELPHIA.

President.—Lieut.-Gen. Philip H. Sheridan.

Soup.
Green Turtle, Sherry Wine.

Fish.
Salmon—Lobster Sauce, Iced Cucumbers, Haut Bareac.

Roast.
Spring Lamb, Mint Sauce.   Fillet de Bœuf, with Mushrooms.
Geisler Blue Seal Champagne.

Vegetables.
Potatoes.   Peas.   Tomatoes.   Cauliflower.

Entrees.
Sweetbreads and Peas.   Chicken Croquettes.

Salad.
Lobster.

Dessert.
Ices.   Meringues.   Fruit.   Claret Wine.   Coffee.
Brandy.   Whiskey.   Cigars.

Toasts.
The President of the U. S.,   . . . Gen. J. S. Fullerton.
George H. Thomas, ... Gen. J. A. Garfield.
The Army and Navy, ... Gen. W. T. Sherman.
The Volunteers, ... Gen. J. P. Bankson.
The Army of the Cumberland, . . . Gen. C. H. Grosvenor.
Sherman's Army, ... Major W. H. Lambert.
Our Departed Comrades,   . . . Gen. Wm. Cogswell.

BANQUET AND RECEPTION TO HON. MATTHEW S. QUAY.

NOVEMBER 23, 1878.

Second only to the entertainment given to Grand Duke Alexis, in 1869, was the reception and banquet tendered to Hon. Matthew S. Quay, late chairman of the Republican State Committee, by the

Union Republican Club, yesterday afternoon and evening, at the clubrooms and banqueting-room of the Continental Hotel. The reception ceremonies commenced promptly at the hour of five o'clock, at the club-rooms, President Addicks officiating, and continued until seven o'clock, when the members of the club to the number of 112, accompanied by twenty-five invited guests, and the grandest display of fireworks ever witnessed in this city, repaired to the banqueting-room of the Continental Hotel.

At precisely eight o'clock the party assembled sat down to the most sumptuous banquet ever prepared in this city, and it was not until 10 o'clock that the lengthy bill of fare was disposed of. At the latter hour Mr. Rufus E. Shapley, the toastmaster of the evening, announced the first toast, to which the honored guest of the occasion, Hon. M. S. Quay, fittingly responded. He was followed by Hon. Morton McMichael, and ex-Governor Thomas L. Young, of Ohio, responded to the toast of "the President of the United States." Governor Hartranft followed, and succeeding him came Governor-elect Hoyt, who, after an excellent speech, introduced General Adam E. King, of Baltimore, who made one of the best speeches of the evening. Hon. Galusha A. Grow followed in a lengthy speech, and he was followed by General Palmer, of Wilkesbarre. Speeches were also made by Colonel Norris and others, until the hour of twelve o'clock arrived, when the party dispersed.

Carl Sentz's band furnished the music for the occasion, while Mr. Murrey superintended the banquet. One of the chief features of the banquet was the bill of fare, which was certainly the handsomest and most costly of any ever gotten up in this city, and, as a souvenir, will long be treasured by all who participated on the occasion.

Prominent among those present were Governor Hartranft, Governor-elect Hoyt, ex-Governor Young, of Ohio, Hon. Galusha A. Grow, Mayor Stokley, ex-Mayor McMichael, Judges Yerkes, Thayer, Briggs, and Ashman, Gen. McCartney, Gen. Palmer, Gen. Owen, Hon. B. H. Brewster, Attorney-General Lear, Hon. Butterworth, First Congressional district of Ohio, Gen. Bingham, James McManes, Esq., United States District-Attorney Valentine, Lieutenant-Governor-elect C. W. Stone, Messrs. Leeds, Hill, Thomas J. Smith, Henry Bumm, and Colonel Norris.

MENU.

Blue Point Oysters.   Chablis.
Green Turtle.   Colbert.
Sherry.
Pates a la Reine.

Salmon Sauce, Hollandaise.
Filet of English Sole, a l'Allemande.   Potato Croquette.
Marcobrunner.
Sweet-Bread, a la Morland.   Breast of Capon, a la Marengo.
Terrapin.   La Rose.
Asparagus, French Peas.   Mumm's Extra Dry.
Punch a la Romaine, in Orange Baskets.
Cigarettes.
Canvas-back Duck.   Saddle of Venison.
Potatoes Parisienne.   Chambertin.
Celery, en Mayonnaise, Lettuce.
Old English and Roquefort Cheese.   Osbourne's Old Port.
Charlotte Russe, Jellies.   Gateaux Assortis Bisquit, Glace.
Ice-Cream, Fruits, French Coffee, Liquors.
—*Judge Bunn's Transcript.*

DINNER A LA MARYLAND.

A patriotic son of Maryland has suggested as a perfect dinner, the choice of the amphitryon being restricted to the productions of the State, the following:

Four small Lynhaven Bay oysters.
Terrapin, a la Maryland.
Canvas-back Duck.
Salad of Crab and Lettuce.
Baked Irish Potatoes.   Fried Hominy Cakes.   Plain Celery.

A royal feast, I assure you; but as I have not been invited, and as the affair may not come off, I feel at liberty to criticise. I consider a salad of crab and lettuce "too heavy" for such a menu as our "patriotic son of Maryland" has suggested; and as for the fried hominy cakes, why, it is like feeding swine on truffles—out of place, I assure you! It is too suggestive of the hog and hominy of the Sunny South. My gastronomic friend, where is your elegant Burgundy, or a bottle of the Leland Brothers' private stock Madeira?

Now I will give you my idea of a loyal dinner:

MENU.
Four Blue Point Oysters.
Consomme with Egg.   Celery.   ·Grated Rusk.
"Petites Bouchees" of Quail.
Terrapin, Philadelphia style.   Saratoga Chips.

Canvas-back Duck.   Currant Jelly.
Lettuce Salad, plain Dressing.
Roquefort Cheese, with Hard Water-Cracker.
Coffee Demi-tasse.

The coffee is to be made at table by an expert; and the wines—well, say a bottle of sparkling Hock made from the Riesling grape served after the soup-plates have been removed, and a choice bottle of good old Burgundy or rare Madeira.

BANQUET TO THE HON. GEORGE LEAR, EX-ATTORNEY-GENERAL, TENDERED BY THE SENATE OF PENNSYLVANIA.

LOCHIEL HOTEL, HARRISBURG, PA., THURSDAY, MARCH 27, 1879.

Served by Thomas J. Murrey, of Continental Hotel, Phila.

MENU.

Oysters.   Celery.   Chablis.
Chicken a la Reine.   Amontillado Sherry.
Petites Bouchees a l'Imperial.
Boiled Striped Bass, Hollandaise.
Broiled Shad, Sauce Tartare.
Cucumber Salad.
P. A. Mumm's Johannesberg.
Fillet of Beef, with Mushrooms.
Loin of Lamb, Epicurean.
Godillat's French Peas.   Potatoes Duchesse.
Chateau La Rose.
Supreme of Fowl, Sauce Bearnaise.
Cutlet of Sweet-breads a la Perigord.
Tomatoes Stuffed au Gratin.
G. H. Mumm's Extra Dry.
Punch Cardinal.   Cigarettes a la Russe.
Squabs Stuffed a la Murrey.   Chambertin.
Lettuce Salad.
Omelette Souffle.   Assorted Jelly.
Glace Napolitaine.   Assorted Cake.
Fruit.
Roquefort Cheese.   Boston Water-Crackers.
Coffee.

A DICKENS CHRISTMAS DINNER.

(From Dickens' Story of "A Christmas Carol.")

COMPOSED BY T. J. MURREY.

Preparatory.

"What's to-day, my fine fellow?" "To-day? why, Christmas day."

The flickering of the blaze showed preparations for a cozy dinner, with hot plates baking through and through before the fire.

She laid the cloth, assisted by Belinda. And everything was good to eat, and in its Christmas dress.

At last the dishes were set on and grace was said.

Dinner.

Oysters.

"Self-contained and solitary as an oyster."

Barrels of Oysters.   Chateau Sauterne.

"A glass of wine ready to our hand."

Light Wine.
Hors-d'œuvre.

Tiny Tim Pickles.

Soup.

Creme of Cauliflower—Fin-Bec.

"The compound was considered perfect."

"It had a remarkable quality, and Scrooge observed it."

Sherry (private stock, 1836).

"From a cask in the merchants' wine-cellars below."

"Here he produced a decanter of wine."

Fish.

Filet of Sole—Sam Ward.

"The very fish in a bowl, though members of a dull and stagnant-blooded race, appeared to know that there was something going on. Scrooge's 'two fish-baskets' never held anything like them."

Boiled Potatoes.

"He blew the fire until the slow potatoes, bubbling up, knocked loudly at the saucepan-lid to be let out and peeled."

Nackenheimer Auslese.

"Satisfactory, too. Oh! perfectly satisfactory."

Valuable Cooking Receipts.

Entree.
Tenderloin of Pork—Chas. Lamb.
"An animal that grunted sometimes."
"Seasonable at Christmas time."

Spanish Onions Stuffed and Baked.
"Shining in the fatness of their growth like Spanish friars."

Pommery Sec.
"Never out of season."
"He iced his."

Punch a la Bishop.
"We will discuss your affairs over the punch."

Roast.
Turkey.
"It is not a fictitious one, glued on a wooden platter."
"Not unlike the big prize turkey that Scrooge sent to the Cratchit family."

Cranberry Sauce.
"Modest tartness."

Goose, Apple Sauce.
Mashed Potato.
"Bob said he didn't believe there ever was such a goose cooked; its tenderness and flavor were the themes of universal satisfaction."
"Eked out by apple-sauce and mashed potato, it was a sufficient dinner for the whole family."

Romanee Conti.
"Came after the roast."
"A noble adjustment of things."

Plain Salad.
"Like lettuce."
"It was made plain enough by the dressing. The 'aromatic vinegar' improved it."

Dessert.
"With the dessert upon the table."

Plum-Pudding, Brandy Sauce.
"Hallo! a great steam! the pudding was out of the copper."
"Mrs. Cratchit entered with a pudding blazing in half a quartern of ignited brandy"
"And a wonderful pudding it was."

Mince-Pies.

"They had mince-pies."

Confections.

"The candied fruits, so caked and spotted with molten sugar as to make the coldest lookers-on feel faint—and subsequently bilious."

Fruit.

"Cherry-cheeked apples and oranges, beseeching to be carried home in paper bags and eaten after dinner."

"There were bunches of grapes, and figs, and raisins, and almonds."

Cheese.

"A crumb of cheese."

Tea and Coffee.

"The blended scents of tea and coffee were so grateful to the nose."

"At last dinner was all done, the cloth was cleared, the 'hot stuff' in the jug was tasted, and Bob proposed—'A Merry Christmas to us all.'"

On Easter day (1880) there was a private banquet at the Rossmore Hotel in this city, prepared, devised, and superintended by Mr. T. J. Murrey. The service was for twenty, and the menu was as follows:

Who can help loving the land that has taught us six hundred and eighty-five ways to dress eggs.—*Moore.*

Oysters.

Wm. Travers once observed that the oyster was a most intelligent creature, since it "shuts up sometimes."

Soup.

Consomme Colbert.

"On holydays, with an egg or two at most."—*Chaucer.*

Fish.

Shad Roe—Bechamel.

"He was as thin as a lath, and lank as a June shad."—W. H. Smith, in the novel of "The Minister's Wife."

Fresh Cucumbers.

"For this, be sure to-night thou shalt have cramps."—*Shakspere.*

Valuable Cooking Receipts.

Relevé.

Leg of Mutton, Caper Sauce.

"It gives true epicures the vapors
To see boiled mutton minus capers."
—Sam Ward.

Entrée.

Puree of Guinea-Hen with Poached Eggs.

"The vulgar boil, the learned poach an egg."—Pope.

Omelette au Rum.

"Made fair in the form of a maiden,
A medley of music and flame."
—Justin McCarthy.

Egg-Nogg, Frappe a l'Alexandria.

Roast.

Squab, stuffed a la Lindenthorpe.

"Like a fat squab upon a Chinese fan."—Cowper.

Green Peas.

"Of the sort that cost some four or five guineas a quart."—Hood.

Baked Potatoes.

"Ireland's native esculent in a baked condition."
—Lord Beaconsfield.

"The principal kind of 'taters' raised by Ireland last year was agitators."—New York *World*, Jan. 18, 1880.

Salad.

Lettuce Francaise.

"Back to the world he'd turn his fleeting soul
And plunge his fingers in the salad bowl."
—Sydney Smith.

Dessert.

Assorted.

"I crack my brains to find out tempting sauces,
And raise fortifications in the pastry."
—Lady Allworth's Cook.

Coffee.

"Mocha's berry from Arabia pure,
  In small, fine China cups, came in at last."
  —Byron.

Cigars.

"Ah! social friend, I love thee well,
  In learned doctors' spite. Thy clouds all other
  Clouds dispel, and lap me in delight."
  —Charles Sprague.

SALAD COLLATION TO GEO. M. TOTTEN, U. S. N.

CONTINENTAL HOTEL, PHILADELPHIA.

Huitres.   Chablis.

Potages.

Colbert.   Cabinet Amontillado.   Pain a Caviar.

Poisson.

Filet de Sole, a la Godard.   Marcobrunner.

Service Froid.

Filet de Bœuf Pique, an Salade Printaniere.   Romance Conti.
  Cotelette de Volaille en Bellevue.
Salade Crabes Dur, a la Gourmand.   Œufs Farci, a la Totten.
  Tartelette de Pigeon, a la Vienna.   Cordon Rouge.
Salad Escarole, a la Murrey.   Celeri.
Laitue.   Fromage de Roquefort.   Old Port (private stock).
Fruit.   Cafe noir.   Liqueurs.

T. J. MURREY, Caterer.
  October 2, 1878.

INDEX.

	PAGE		PAGE
Antiseptic	113	Cake, Ginger Cup	79
App'e Sauce	110	Icing	79
Snow	76	English Christmas	75
Toddy, Hot	107	Knickerbocker	77
Arrowroot for Batters and Sauces	37	Lady Fingers, No. 1	80
Artichokes, Boiled	92	" " No. 2	81
Jerusalem	92	Macaroons	79
Asparagus, Boiled	92	Maids of Honor	81
Banquet Service	101	Marbled	80
Beef a la Mode	21	Neapolitan	80
Corned	18	Pound, without Soda	80
Fillet of	20	Olive Gingerbread	77
Roast	39	Whortleberry, No. 1	78
Beets, Boiled	95	" " No. 2	78
Biscuit, Milk	61	Windsor	79
Blanc-Mange	82	Zephyr	77
Boiling, Remarks on	17	Calf's Brains en Matelotte	23
Bread, How to make	59	" Fried	24
Boston Brown	61	" and Tongue	24
Steamed "	61	Head	22
Corn	60	" Broiled	23
Continental Hotel Corn	61	" Collared	23
Wheat	60	" Fried	22
Stuffing	46	" Maitre d'Hotel	23
Cabbage, Remarks on	91	Capon, Boiled	20
Cake, Corn	62	Roast	46
Fried Bread	62	Carrots	94
Almond	76	Cauliflower, Boiled	95
Almond Sponge	76	Celery, Boiled	94
Chocolate	77	Champagne	104
Chocolate Macaroons	78	Charlotte Russe	81
Cocoanut	77	Chestnut Stuffing	45
Cocoanut Pound	78	Chickens a l'Italienne	29
Columbia	77	Boiled	19
Cream	79	Croquettes	29
Crescents	81	Fricassee	28

Index.

	PAGE		PAGE
Chickens, Fried	29	Ice Cream, Lemon	85
Liver en Brochette	31	Peach	85
Patties	30	Vanilla	85
Panada	30	Ices, Water, Apricot	85
Pie	30	" Lemon	85
Roast	46	Icing for Cake	79
Roast Prairie	49	Jam	110
Toast	31	Jelly, Currant	110
With Dumplings	31	Wine	110
With Rice	29	Kettles, Preparing for use	113
Cider, How to keep fresh	110	Lamb, Breast of	28
Codfish, Baked	12	Fricassee	28
Salt, with Cream	13	Roast	41
Coffee, Remarks on	86	Roast Saddle of	41
Corn, Boiled	95	Lemonade	106
Cream, Bavarian	83	Lobster, Broiled	13
Ice	84	En Brochette	14
Italian	83	Macaroni, Baked	34
Lemon Ice	85	Macaroons	79
Manioca	82	Basket	83
Peach Ice	85	Chocolate	78
Vanilla Ice	85	Mackerel, Salt, Broiled	13
Whipped Coffee	83	Meringues	82
Whipped with Liqueurs	83	Milk Punch	106
Crullers	69	Mince Meat for Pies	65
Cucumber, Stewed	96	Mixed Drinks	106
Dandelion, Stewed	96	Muffins, Continental Hotel	61
Dressing, Plain French	52	Mushrooms, Remarks on	58
Plain English	53	Mutton, Remarks on	40
Bacon	53	Boiled Leg of	18
Duck, Braise of, with Turnips	31	Breast of, with Peas	25
Braise of, with Peas	31	Curry of	26
Roast Canvas-Back	48	Hash with Poached Eggs	26
Roast Domestic	47	Pie	27
Wild, Salmé of	32	Ragout of	26
Drinks, Mixed	106	Roast Leg of	41
Dyspepsia Cure	113	Roast Loin of	41
Eels, Fricasseed	14	Omelettes, Remarks on	37
Patties	15	Oyster	38
Egg-Nogg	106	Rum	38
Egg-Plant, Stuffed, No. 1	25	Souffle	38
Stuffed, No. 2	35	Onions	94
Etiquette, Table	97	Orange Basket	86
Fritters	37	Oyster-Plant	95
Golden Buck	39	Croquettes	36
Goose, Roast	47	Stuffing	46
Ham à la Russe	48	Oysters, à la Poulette	7
Boiled	19	Broiled	7
Horse Radish, Boiled	96	Escalloped	6
Hot Apple Toddy	107	Fried	7
Spiced Rum	107	Patties	6
Tom and Jerry	107	Raw	5
Ice Cream, How to make	84	Roast on half-shell	6

Index.

	PAGE		PAGE
Oysters, Roast	7	Punch, Santa Cruz	107
Parsnip Fritters	36	Preserving	108
Partridge, Salmé of	32	Quail, Roast	49
Paste	64	Quinces, Canning	112
Peas, Green	93	Rail-Birds	49
" Bottled	93	Rarebit, Welsh	38
Pickle, Green Tomato	112	" Yorkshire	39
Pies, Remarks on	62	Reed-Birds	50
Apple	64	Rice Croquettes	34
" Meringue	65	Roasting, Remarks on	30
" Sliced	64	Salads, Remarks on	51
" Custard	65	Alligator Pear	58
Beefsteak	21	Asparagus	56
Custard	66	Chicken	55
Fruit	66	Cucumber and Tomato	57
Lemon Cream, No. 1	66	Cucumber	57
" " No. 2	67	Herring	55
Orange	67	Hop Sprouts	56
Pumpkin	66	Lettuce	52
Pigeon, Roast	47	Lobster	54
Pork, Remarks on	42	Muskmelon	58
and Beans	33	Potato	55
Chops, Tomato Sauce	24	Sandwich	57
Sausages	25	Turnip Tops	56
Potatoes, Remarks on	90	Veal	55
Balls	35	Salmon, Soyer's Boiled	15
Cakes	36	Salt, Remarks on	58
Fritters	36	Santa Cruz Punch	107
Stuffed	35	Sauces, Anchovy	16
Powder, Baking	70	Celery	16
Puff Paste	63	Caper	16
Pudding, Almond	72	Chili	112
Astor House	74	Drawn Butter	15
Bachelor's	73	Dutch	17
Batter	69	Egg	17
Bird's Nest	73	Hot	112
Boiled	68	Lobster	16
Citron	74	Maitre d'Hotel	15
Chocolate	69	Mint	41
Cocoanut	73	Mayonnaise, No. 1	53
Eve's	74	" No. 2	53
Harlan's	73	Oyster, No. 1	16
Manhattan	75	" No. 2	17
Manioca	75	Robert	25
Macaroni	72	Summer Mayonnaise	53
Marlborough	72	Tartare	23
Plum, English	67	Tomato	25
" Plain	68	Vanilla	69
" New England	68	Vinaigrette	53
Roly-Poly	71	Wine	73
" Lemon	71	Gravy for baked Fish	17
Sliced Apple	74	For Plum-Pudding	68
Steamed Arrowroot	72	Shad, Baked	14

Index.

	PAGE		PAGE
Sherries	108	Tonic, Morning	113
Snipe, Roast	49	Tongue, Boiled	19
Soup, Beef Tea	11	Tripe, Broiled	33
Chicken, No. 1	11	Fricassee	33
" No. 2	11	Lyonnaise	33
Gumbo	8	Trout Tenderloin	14
Mock Turtle	9	Turkey, Remarks on	14
Ox Tail	10	Boiled	19
Pea	10	Roast	45
" Economical	10	Turnips, Boiled	93
Stock	8	Veal Croquettes	27
Tomato	10	Fricassee of	27
Veal Stock	8	Roast Loin of	40
" Broth	8	Venison, Breast of	33
Spiced Rum, Hot	107	Chops	32
Spinach, Boiled	94	Epicurean	32
Sprouts, Brussels	93	Patties	33
Stew, Beef	21	Roast	48
Sweetbreads, Stewed	24	Weeds	97
Table Etiquette	97	Whiskies	108
Tomatoes, Canning	112	Wines, Remarks on	102
Stuffed	34	Woodcock, Roast	49
Tom and Jerry, Hot	107		

www.ingramcontent.com/pod-product-compliance
Lightning Source LLC
Chambersburg PA
CBHW020110170426
43199CB00009B/475